Your Towns and Cities in the Gre

Shrewsbury
in the Great War

Your Towns and Cities in the Great War

Shrewsbury
in the Great War

Dorothy Nicolle

Pen & Sword
MILITARY

First published in Great Britain in 2015 by
PEN & SWORD MILITARY
an imprint of
Pen and Sword Books Ltd
47 Church Street
Barnsley
South Yorkshire S70 2AS

ISBN 978 1 78383 113 5

A CIP record for this book is available from the British Library.

Printed and bound in England
by CPI Group (UK) Ltd, Croydon, CR0 4YY

Typeset in Times New Roman

Pen & Sword Books Ltd incorporates the imprints of
Pen & Sword Archaeology, Atlas, Aviation, Battleground, Discovery,
Family History, History, Maritime, Military, Naval, Politics, Railways,
Select, Social History, Transport, True Crime, and Claymore Press,
Frontline Books, Leo Cooper, Praetorian Press, Remember When,
Seaforth Publishing and Wharncliffe.
For a complete list of Pen and Sword titles please contact
Pen and Sword Books Limited
47 Church Street, Barnsley, South Yorkshire, S70 2AS, England
E-mail: enquiries@pen-and-sword.co.uk
Website: **www.pen-and-sword.co.uk**

Contents

Abbreviations used in the book:

Chronicle	*Shrewsbury Chronicle* newspaper
DORA	The Defence of the Realm Act
KSLI	King's Shropshire Light Infantry
MAB	Metropolitan Asylums Board
VAD	Voluntary Aid Detachment

Dedication

Wars are not just about the soldiers who fight. Those who wait at home suffer too. This book is particularly dedicated to those who stay at home during war time, the families and friends of the fighting men, who in their own way also serve their country.

Chapter One

A brief history of Shrewsbury

THROUGHOUT ITS HISTORY the town of Shrewsbury has known much of war. Its very position, sitting on a hilltop site and surrounded by the natural moat of the River Severn, tells us that the first people who settled here had the threat of warfare and the need for defence very much on their minds.

We don't know when the first people settled here. When the Romans first arrived nearly two thousand years ago they found the region was already occupied by a warlike people, the Celts, who had established hill forts that dotted the landscape. From such fortified positions individual tribes could watch over their own territories and that of neighbouring tribes – always ready to grab any opportunity to raid their neighbours' cattle.

Then the Romans arrived. They had no need of the protection afforded by forts strategically placed on the tops of hills. Their strength was in their legions and the psychological terror such efficient soldiers inflicted on the people they overran. So it was that when the Romans established a legionary base they chose a low-lying site near the banks of the River Severn some four miles east of Shrewsbury, a site that we now know as Wroxeter. As time passed the legions moved on, first to Chester and then to northern England and relative peace descended on the region.

This peace lasted for several hundred years but was eventually torn apart by the arrival of a new breed of warrior-people – the Anglo-Saxons – and it was they who chose the site we now know as Shrewsbury. Those Saxons chose well. A hill-top site, presumably with some form of palisade or ramparts around it, almost completely surrounded by river and what would, in those days, have been pretty soggy, permanent

The Roman ruins at Wroxeter.

Shrewsbury Castle.

THE CASTLE, SHREWSBURY.

marshland. Even the town's name reminds us that this was a carefully chosen and fortified site. The *bury* element in Shrewsbury tells us that this was a burgh town, a fortified town. And it needed to be.

Shrewsbury was the new settlement established by an invading group and therefore needed protection from attack from the natives whom they had displaced – those Welsh people, as they came to be known. Indeed, even the name *Welsh* comes from a Saxon word that meant *foreigner* which is a bit cheeky really, when you come to think of it because it was the Saxons who were the real foreigners.

And so, for the next few hundred years an uneasy truce (with regular interruptions as the two groups raided each others livestock) would have been the customary way of life for anyone living here. Until the arrival of the next invaders – the Normans.

The Normans set about a systematic domination of the nation they had just defeated. In Shrewsbury Roger de Montgomery built a castle; it was one of a whole series that protected the English-Welsh border – those Welsh were still proving to be troublesome and were to remain so for the next few hundred years. In fact their attacks on the town were such a regular feature of life that in the 1240s King Henry

Medieval tower on Town Walls.

III decreed that whatever protection the town had at that time was insufficient and proper stone walls should be built. Stretches of this wall still survive along with one tower.

From then on Shrewsbury became more of a base from where English armies could depart on campaigns into the Welsh hills. It's an indication of just how secure the Shrewsbury people felt once these walls had been built when one considers that within some forty or so years, they were already building houses abutting those walls. Doing this must inevitably have impeded access along the walls for defenders in times of attack and yet it was still allowed.

With the Welsh held in check beyond their borders and the only real fighting for professional soldiers taking place in France the Shrewsbury people settled down to what they did best – trading – and Shrewsbury prospered. It became a major market centre for the region and the wealth of those centuries can still be seen in the fine old timber buildings that adorn the town.

But life wasn't without its troubles. In the year 1403 Shrewsbury was to be the scene of a major battle between King Henry IV and the rebel Henry Percy, son of the Earl of Northumberland, who is generally better known as Harry Hotspur. Just a couple of miles to the north of the town the two armies met on 21 July. Parleys were held but none of the main protagonists really wanted to avoid a fight and so the battle began at around four o'clock that afternoon. It lasted for some three or so hours and at the end of that time probably somewhere in the range of 6,000 men lay dead or dying.

The Battle of Shrewsbury was not an important battle historically. It never changed a dynasty; indeed, it could be said to have confirmed Henry IV's position as king since he had usurped the throne some four years before. On the other hand, it was an extremely important battle militarily. This was the first battle fought on English soil where both sides used the longbow – to devastating effect. Moreover, the

Statue of Henry IV on Battlefield Church.

teenage son of the king could be said to have been well and truly blooded here – he was the future King Henry V, the future victor of the Battle of Agincourt. And blooded he certainly was, being wounded in the face by an arrow.

The end of the 1400s almost saw another battle in the town. In this case, in 1485, Shrewsbury was threatened by Henry Tudor who, accompanied by his army, was on his

Battlefield Church.

Henry Tudor House on Wyle Cop.

way to meet King Richard III at Bosworth Field. On demanding entry into the town he was first refused but, subsequently, he was allowed in for fear of the damage his army would undoubtedly cause if they had to fight their way in.

Following his victory at Bosworth Field Henry Tudor became King Henry VII; under him England and Wales became linked and a further 150 years of peace descended on the town.

And then, in 1642 King Charles I raised his standard in Nottingham and so began the Civil War. It wasn't long before war came to Shrewsbury, first of all in the guise of the king himself, seeking money to fund his campaign. He borrowed from Shrewsbury School (it's a debt that has never been repaid, incidentally), he billeted his men on households throughout the town (which inevitably caused annoyance) and he had the castle refortified.

Finally, in February 1645, the Parliamentarians attacked. The town was taken relatively easily and ever since then debate has raged as to whether or not there was a traitor within the walls who opened the gate at the bottom of St Mary's Water Lane. (The street has been known locally as Traitor's Gate ever since, which does seem to lend some credence to the tale.) Whatever the truth of the matter, several hostages were captured at the castle and subsequently executed but, here too, there seems to be controversy. Tradition has it that the executed soldiers were *Irish* but no-one seems sure as to just what this means – were they Irish men fighting for the King's cause or Royalist soldiers who had fought in Ireland?

One Shrewsbury man who was involved in the capture of Shrewsbury was Captain John Benbow. As a Parliamentarian sympathizer he had joined the army and so, with his local knowledge, was one of the leaders in the attack on the town. Subsequently, however, King Charles I was captured and then executed in January 1649. The execution of an anointed king appalled people throughout the country and caused many Parliamentarians to change sides. Captain Benbow was one who changed his allegiances so that, two years later, he was fighting for the Royalist cause at the Battle of Worcester. The last battle of the Civil War, it was a disaster for the Royalists. Benbow was captured and, inevitably, considered a traitor for having changed sides. He was brought back to Shrewsbury and executed by firing squad in front of the entrance to Shrewsbury Castle. His grave is to be found in the churchyard of Old St Chad's Church.

Once again calm descended and from this period on any militaristic associations that there are with the town are through those of its men who either joined the British forces or who passed through the town at some point in their lives. One of the latter was Judge George Jeffreys – notorious as the judge who oversaw the Bloody Assizes following the Monmouth Rebellion in 1685. He quickly became known as the Hanging Judge – on one day alone he condemned nearly 100 people to death. His association with Shrewsbury, however, is only slight – he attended Shrewsbury School for a short time.

Another, who like Jeffreys was not a Shrewsbury man, was Thomas Anderson. Anderson was a Yorkshire man with Jacobite sympathies at the time of Bonnie Prince Charlie's rebellion in 1745. Despite this he had joined the British army but then went absent without leave and was eventually captured in Edinburgh. By this time the regiment with which he was supposed to be serving was based in Shrewsbury and so he was brought to the town for his court martial, after which he was executed. Feelings against Jacobites were running high at the time so that, when his body was brought to St Mary's Church for burial not only did his fellow soldiers refuse to carry his body into the church but neither were the local people prepared to do so. Despite this he was buried in the churchyard.

A contemporary of Anderson's was a man whose reputation ran high for many years – although these days it is deemed politically incorrect to praise him. I speak of Robert Clive,

St Mary's Water Lane, known locally as Traitor's Gate.

St Mary's Church.

conqueror of India. Imperialism is a bad word nowadays and people tend to forget that it was not just the British who had imperialistic ideas in the eighteenth and nineteenth centuries. In India in the mid-1700s both the British and the French (each of them supported by different Indian factions) were in India fighting each other for supremacy in what both countries saw as the potential jewel in a future empire. If India had not become part of a British Empire it would have been part of a French one instead.

French ambitions turned to Europe instead, particularly following the rise of Napoleon Bonaparte. One Shropshire general, whose deteriorating statue still looks over the town, was Rowland Hill. Joining the army at the age of eighteen, Hill rose through the ranks so that by the time of the Peninsular Wars he was a general and it was there that his reputation was really established. He became Wellington's right-hand-man and was the one general Wellington always felt he could rely on. Second-in-Command (under Wellington) at the Battle of Waterloo he was thought at one time to have been killed when his horse was shot under him. He survived, however, and subsequently became Commander-in-Chief of the British Army.

And so, throughout its history the town of Shrewsbury has known much of war. But when war came in 1914 it was to be like nothing that had ever affected the townspeople before.

Lord Rowland Hill's Column.   **Robert Clive of India.**

Chapter Two

The Calm before the Storm

WHEN THE YEAR 1914 dawned there was no-one who imagined just what lay ahead. Certainly there were parts of the world where there was unrest, the Balkans obviously, but recent problems in Russia seemed to have calmed down. Kaiser Wilhelm II in Germany was posturing as usual, but by now other countries around the globe had become somewhat accustomed to this and generally ignored his pretensions. France was still smarting after the failure of the Franco-Prussian War some forty years before and was gearing up, preparing for 'Part Two' of that fiasco, but that would just be between them and Germany. Surely.

Certainly, no-one foresaw a war on the scale that was about to come.

In the United Kingdom little notice was taken of events and squabbles in the rest of Europe. This was a period that saw increasing emigration from Britain to its colonies around the world. Newspapers of the time were full of articles extolling the virtues of life in Canada or Australia alongside advertisements for the shipping lines that would take you to these and other such places. Wages for farm workers in these countries were good – from £1 to 25 shillings a week with free board and lodging – and prospects for the future were excellent. There were even occasional advertisements from men who had already emigrated and now sought wives to join them in the colonies.

Within the British Isles the question of Home Rule for the Irish was a subject of abiding interest. As it happened, once war was declared Home Rule for Ireland was put

Shrewsbury High Street

Wyle Cop - notice the herd of cattle being driven down the street.

on the back-burner of political importance until (that is) two years later when it erupted with violence in the Easter Rebellion.

Another subject of prime interest to Britons at the time was the question of women's suffrage. The suffragettes were not just marching under Mrs Pankhurst in London. Or even in Britain. In the United States President Woodrow Wilson spoke out against women's suffrage in Congress whilst in a court room in Paris one lady, when asked by the judge what she could possibly do in public life looked at the dirty windows which were covered with cobwebs and, to much amusement, stated, 'The first thing we shall do will be to have those windows cleaned, and to make public rooms look decent.'

In Shrewsbury, then and in the war years that followed, there were regular lectures on the subject of votes for women, with men and women on both sides of the argument. But this, too, was a subject that was put on a political back-burner once war was declared. Of course, in many respects, it was the war and the part played by women during it, that was to give women the vote by the time an election was called at the end of 1918.

The British Empire, problems in Ireland, women's suffrage were all subjects that interested the people of Shrewsbury in the early years of the twentieth century but, by and large, it was subjects closer to home that were of most interest.

Shrewsbury at the start of 1914 was a thriving country market town with a population of a little over 50,000. The town sat in the middle of a largely rural community that covered not just Shropshire but also extended into western Wales. There were regular weekly markets – the Smithfield market (in Raven Meadows) was large enough depending on the livestock being sold for some 700 horses or 4,000 head of cattle, 7,000 sheep or 1,000 pigs. There were three breweries in the town, along with tanneries and timber yards. There was industry, too, with an iron foundry that primarily supplied agricultural implements.

Highlights of the year for Shrewsbury people at the time included things like the annual flower show, regattas held by Shrewsbury School and, particularly in 1914, the agricultural show. The show was to be held that year between 30 June and 4 July and early on rumours started to circulate that King George V and Queen Mary would attend, making it a Royal Agricultural Show. The joy of the townspeople when this news was confirmed was overwhelming. There was, of course, the problem of finding the funding to pay for such a visit so that the Mayor asked for donations from the general public (of well over £1,000) to cover the cost of decorating the town.

It was on 3 July that the king and queen arrived for a visit that lasted only four hours. They processed from Shrewsbury Station, through streets that were lined with people. Their route took them to the Square where they were formally welcomed by the Mayor. Whilst there King George laid a foundation stone for Shrewsbury School's new library despite the fact that the school was some distance away. The Head Boy, Francis Kinchin-Smith, presented King George with a model of the foundations; the king (still sitting in his carriage) pressed a switch and a miniature stone dropped into position. From the Square the royal couple then went on to the show ground on the racecourse at Monkmoor where they were driven past groups of veteran soldiers and even a long line of prize bulls which included a champion Dexter that the king himself owned. (Francis Kinchin-Smith,

Post card produced to celebrate King George's visit. *(David Benson)*

incidentally, survived the war although he was wounded and became a PoW.)

While he was in Shrewsbury King George made a speech in which he described Shrewsbury as 'an ancient and picturesque town… once the scene of many famous battles… [but now] a flourishing centre of peaceful pursuits'.

Such was the excitement of the Shrewsbury people over their monarch's visit that little else was talked about for days afterwards. So it is perhaps no surprise that an assassination that took place in Sarajevo a few days before the show opened was not considered important enough to be given even a brief mention in the local paper.

King George lays the foundation stone. *(Shrewsbury School)*

Chapter Three

War Breaks Out

THERE HAD BEEN trouble in the Balkans for years but no-one in Britain really took much notice. The spark that lit the fuse, however, occurred on 28 June when a Serbian revolutionary named Gavrilo Princip shot and killed the heir to the Austro-Hungarian throne, Archduke Franz Ferdinand, and his wife as they drove through the streets of Sarajevo. Still, no-one in Britain took much notice.

It wasn't until almost a month later when news arrived at the Foreign Office in London that, urged on by the German Kaiser, the Austrian Emperor had issued an ultimatum to Serbia insisting that they, the Austrians, should control any inquiry into the assassination and also that Serbia should suppress all anti-Austrian propaganda within the country along with several other demands. Although the Serbians agreed to all but one of the Austrian demands, this single refusal was all that Austria wanted and so war was declared between the two states the following day. It was only then that the British government (until then almost wholly absorbed with Irish affairs) began to take notice and in the days that followed the unsteady house of cards that was based on alliances, some of which were decades old, began to collapse.

No sooner had Austria-Hungary declared war on Serbia than Russia, under Tsar Nicholas II, came in to support 'little Serbia'. This gave Germany's Kaiser, Wilhelm II, the opportunity he sought and so he threatened that if Russia's allies, France and Britain, did not curb Russia then he would have to intervene. Russia was not prepared to back down and so Germany, too, mobilized. Inevitably, France followed suit, war being declared between the two on 3 August.

His army already mobilized, Kaiser Wilhelm's plan was to invade France as quickly as possible. Anticipating such an attack would come at sometime, the French had long since built up fortifications along their border with Germany. This left their border with Belgium relatively undefended and it was here that Germany planned to invade, passing through Belgium along the way. The German government therefore sent an ultimatum to Belgium demanding to be allowed to move through Belgian territory unhindered. The Belgians refused and the German army poured in.

It was an almost-forgotten Treaty of London that had been signed in 1839 that then brought Britain into the fracas. Belgium had then been a newly independent country and this independence (together with Belgium's neutrality) had been guaranteed by the United Kingdom. And so, it was Germany's invasion of Belgium that brought Britain into the war on 4 August.

It was a Bank Holiday weekend and the Government quickly did two things. Firstly they extended the holiday by an additional day to prevent a run on the banks and then they rapidly passed the Defence of the Realm Act (DORA) which, as additional rulings were added, was to give the Government wide-ranging powers. Everything from flying kites, to buying binoculars, to the requisition of property and, probably best-known today, the licensing hours of pubs, were amongst the many new regulations brought in under DORA in the years that followed.

In Shrewsbury, just as it was in the rest of the country, the news was generally welcomed. Germany had for some years been threatening Britain's imperial interests and this would give the country an opportunity to deal with the upstart once and for all, was the attitude of many.

Despite the fact that the actual declaration of war had come as such a surprise, things moved remarkably quickly. War was declared on a Tuesday; the following day the mobilization of the Shropshire Light Infantry was such that, by that same evening, already 160 men were leaving the town to join the 1st Battalion which was then stationed in Tipperary, Ireland and, to speed up the process, a special platform had, even then, been erected on the Castle Foregate side of Shrewsbury Station to enable guns and horses to be more easily entrained.

A CHIP OF THE OLD BLOCK.

'A chip of the old block'.

Within days posters appeared on signboards and advertisements in all the newspapers urging men to join up and advising them just how to do so. It was August, the harvest had almost been gathered in – and so men were told that it was now their duty to sign up as soon as the harvest was in. And they did. Many assumed that they would be home 'by Christmas', after all, and ready once again to work in the fields when they were needed in the spring. It was this kind of thinking that encouraged many soldiers to sign up 'for the duration' as opposed to a specified time, little realizing, of course, just how long they were thus committing themselves for.

Before long the lack of men meant that a number of businesses were finding themselves understaffed and so shops began to restrict their opening times, usually by closing the doors for an hour at lunch time. The tone of advertisements in the *Situations Vacant* columns soon changed with potential employers now looking for a strong youth or lad where before they would have wanted adults.

Recruiting meetings became a regular feature within the town and at any public event there would be people present urging young men to volunteer. The whole thing would often have an almost party feel to it, a band would be playing, stirring speeches would be made. But it didn't always work – there are regular comments in the *Shrewsbury Chronicle* decrying the fact that the response to such an event was disappointing.

White Feathers

Right from the beginning men were made to feel that it was their patriotic duty to fight. Posters and cartoon illustrations in the papers showed scenes where children asked their father *What did you do in the war, Daddy?* or *We don't want to lose you, but we think you ought to go* was a prevailing feeling amongst many women. Indeed, women were made to feel that they should encourage their men. *If he does not think that you and your country are worth fighting for – do you think he is worthy of you?* asked one such poster.

Before long men who weren't in uniform were made to feel uncomfortable, to say the very least. *Slackers* or *shirkers* as they were often described were derided in the streets and in the press. Every one wanted to comment so that the following exhortation, which is typical of many,

What would have been a familiar sign on hoardings in the years leading up to the war.

was printed in the *St Mary's Church Parish Magazine*: 'amid so much of what is good and splendid it is sad to see the number of hale and hearty young men who are still hanging back from enlisting. I do not refer to those who are prohibited by health or any other sound reason, but I do mean those who deliberately do not intend to go until they are fetched. They ought to be thoroughly ashamed of themselves; they should be tabooed and ostracized by every decent person. They ought to be made to feel that they are not wanted here, and that the sooner they relieve us of their company the better... The very sight of them as they lounge about our town is sickening, and I only hope they understand how contemptible they are in the eyes of every patriotic man and woman.'

Those families whose sons had joined up (often in large numbers) were held up as an example to the slackers. The Parish Magazine for St Michael's Church in Ditherington approached the subject slightly differently from St Mary's vicar but the message in the end was much the same. 'Our young men,' the vicar in Ditherington wrote, 'are rolling up well – four sons of one family have joined; three sons of another. There still remain a few who will, we hope, join before they "may be fetched"'.

As time passed and mortality lists began to grow, the message became starker. The first anniversary of the outbreak of war produced a number of advertisements aimed at the men who still had not volunteered: 'We have been at war a year. Thousands of brave men have shed their blood for you – they have made their sacrifice willingly, compelled, not by law, but by sense of duty, to offer to their country all the best they had to give. What have you done in return?... Will you play the game

PATRIOTIC SAYINGS:

THE VALIANT FEW MUST SUFFER FOR THE BETTERMENT OF THE LAND

Photos by J. Russell & Sons.

Post card reminding people of their duty.

or let your comrades down? Or are you smugly waiting to be fetched?' went one such advertisement.

It wasn't long before men who were not in uniform, or obviously wounded and incapable, would be given white feathers. In fact, the white feather as a symbol of cowardice dates back to the eighteenth century when cockfighting was still popular – the best fighting birds were gamecocks and it was thought that those birds with white feathers in their tails would be poor fighters. The practice of giving men in civvies white feathers in order to shame them into enlisting proved to be very effective; it also caused a great deal of outrage when the recipients of feathers turned out to be soldiers home on leave, men who were wounded but not obviously so, or men working for the war effort in some other way. Indeed it became such a problem that the government saw a need eventually to issue those men working for the war effort but still civilians with lapel badges that read *King and Country*.

Nagging and taunting of young, still under-age, men who looked older than their years also caused many problems. When the war was first declared and aged only sixteen one such lad had volunteered in the Royal Horse Artillery and been accepted by them when he claimed that he was already nineteen. His parents, however, had managed to get him out of the army. Looking older than his years, he was constantly teased and finally, in order to stop everyone jeering at him, he forged a certificate to show that he had been discharged as medically unfit. He ended up in court in Shrewsbury accused of forging the certificate in order to avoid the attention of recruiting officers which, of course, had never been his intention. He was still only seventeen and, thus, still under-age but he was ready to join up as soon as he was old enough, he told the court. He was fined £3.

It wasn't just with white feathers that young, apparently fit and able men were taunted. As early as August 1914 an advertisement appeared in *The Times* that read: 'Wanted petticoats for able young men who have not yet joined the army.'

Perhaps it was this that gave one lady who lived in Frankwell the idea. With two sons of her own who had joined up and a husband working for the military she was frustrated by the sight of one of her young neighbours who had failed to join up and she would regularly give the 'supposed shirker' a piece of her mind, as it was reported in the *Chronicle*. Then one day she finally lost her temper and waving a petticoat over her head she chased him down the street shouting 'You ought to wear these.' I wonder if he did then join up.

By 1916 the search for shirkers was now being pressed vigorously, but many men still escaped the net of the recruiting officers. It was difficult to hide in a town the size of Shrewsbury, easier in a place like Liverpool where, according to one report young men had got jobs as night taxi drivers. 'The recruiting officers are busy in the day-time, but one is safe in the dark hours. I know a number who have escaped,' said one envious man.

Chapter Four

The Arrival of the Belgian Refugees

IT WAS THE German invasion of Belgium that was the final straw that caused war to be declared as the United Kingdom had, as long ago as 1839, guaranteed the independence of the new state when it had been formed. Within days Belgians were fleeing their country and seeking refuge in the Netherlands and in France. Many of them subsequently came to Britain. A census of the number of Belgians in Britain in 1917 counted over 170,000 although the actual number was probably far greater.

German infantry in Belgium in the summer of 1914.
(Taylor Library)

Belgian refugees resting beside the road during their flight. *(Taylor Library)*

On their arrival in England many of the refugees found themselves being looked after by the Metropolitan Asylums Board (MAB). This charitable institution had been founded in 1867 to look after, not just the mentally sick despite its name, but also the poor of London particularly during times of epidemics.

Soon after the war broke out the MAB took over the Earl's Court Exhibition buildings. It's an indication of the efficiency of the organization that an exhibition closed one evening and the next evening the place was ready to accept some 400 refugees. Within a week there were 2,000 men, women and children camping in vast dormitories there. Obviously people could not stay there permanently and so arrangements were made to transfer the refugees to homes around the country.

By now the newspapers were full of stories about the atrocities being meted out by the Germans as they overran Belgium and so offers of accommodation came raining in. But not all were suitable.

Quite a few Belgians came to Shropshire and throughout the county there were many groups who did their best to help the refugees to settle in. One building that was used in Shrewsbury was the Armoury on Victoria Quay which was requisitioned by the government for use as a hostel. Such accommodation wasn't ideal, especially for families with children and so alternative housing was sought in the surrounding countryside.

When things go well and people blend in with their fellows, find work and generally get themselves back on their own feet, little tends to be said about them. It's when there are problems that you hear of individual cases and, fortunately, in the Shrewsbury

**The Armoury,
Victoria Avenue.**

Archives there is a collection of carbon copies of letters sent by one gentleman, Mr Everest, who was taking care of the refugees. Writing from his office in St John's Hill he busily arranged housing, found jobs, replaced pairs of boots and generally tried to keep the peace between warring families. His letters, of course, just give one side of the conversation but are fascinating nevertheless. They start in November 1914.

In order to obtain a degree of independence people need work but there were problems here because the Belgians stuck in the overcrowded Earl's Court accommodation would often say they had any qualifications just to get away from there. Then, when he tried to get jobs for the Belgians through the Shrewsbury Labour Exchange, Mr Everest found that they made offers of work below regular English rates which were totally unfair and so he ended up placing them in work himself.

But what Mr Everest really wanted was people who could work in the nearby farms. He wanted peasants or, as he sometimes refers to them, agriculturalists, and he frequently complains in letters to his colleagues that he's being sent the wrong type of people. In a letter in December he wrote 'there were no peasants among the 32 sent. You will notice in my letter of the 4th inst that I stipulated most clearly that the refugees must be of the peasant class.

'Those you have sent me are apparently a very nice lot but they are superior to the class for which I have accommodation. I know your difficulties and will try to help you by placing this lot but please do not send me any more at present because I do not know how long it will take me to deal with these.'

A couple of days later he was arranging a swop with the refugee office in Oswestry – he would get a family of peasants in exchange for a butcher/hotel proprietor and his family.

Not all the Belgian families got on. There was one family in particular that caused trouble for Mr Everest when they had to share a cottage. He wrote in a letter:

'I am sorry, but the Steeman's family seem very unhappy. They say that the Van Aken's believe that they (the Steemans) are there to obey their orders and they beg very pitifully that the Committee will either put them with some other family or by themselves. They go so far as to say that they would rather go back to Earl's Court with all its discomforts, than remain with the Van Akens. I think you will agree with me that we should be doing wrong to leave them there in the circumstances. I blame myself for arranging to mix Malinoise with other Belgians because I had so many warnings about the people from Maline but I thought your family looked so much superior to others.'

Apparently, up and down the country people from Maline (present-day Mechelen) were causing problems and in another letter, this time to a colleague working in Harrogate, Mr Everest returned to the subject:

'We find for some reason which we cannot explain that it is absolutely impossible to put Malinoise and other Belgians together. It does not seem to matter what class the Malinoise are, the other refugees cannot hit it off. I cannot find any explanation for this which is satisfactory. The Flemish priests say that the people of Maline are socialists but this does not explain the difficulty as I have found socialists and anti-clericals from other parts of Belgium who can get on very well with devout Catholics. Other Belgians have described the Malinoise as "a town of rag gatherers" but this also does not solve the curious problem, as we have had some very decent people from Malines. Have you come across the same trouble, and if so have you fathomed the cause of it?'

One aspect of his work that obviously gave Mr Everest a great deal of pleasure was reuniting families that had become separated as they fled from Belgium. In one case he found the mother of two young girls who had somehow made their way to Shropshire:

'You will remember the two Van Dessell girls. I advertised for their mother and I am sure you will be pleased to know that I have found her and am getting in touch with her. One does not mind any amount of work with results like these.'

But that wasn't the end of the story because, having found the girls' mother he discovered that she was living with her brother and so he asked his colleague in Devizes,

'will you please let me know whether Madame's brother is a decent fellow. If he is, I think we would be glad to arrange to take the whole family and put them into a cottage.'

Happily, the brother turned out to be 'a decent fellow'. Another pleasure that he had was arranging for a Christmas celebration for the refugees and so he firstly sent letters out to colleagues in the area asking them to count the number of children needing gifts and then, when arranging a lunch for adults, asked for a head count to be made at the Roman Catholic church on Town Walls.

Men of military age were expected, like those in Britain, to join up although in their case in the Belgian Army. Not all wanted to go. So, once again, he wrote to the Belgian priest, Father de Ryk:

The Roman Catholic Cathedral, Town Walls.

'I regret to say the Van Steenes refuse to join the Army and say that if they are ordered to do so they will injure themselves. No doubt a talk from you to-morrow will put them in a better frame of mind but, if not, they will be sent to one of the Concentration camps in London.'

The following week the two men had agreed to sign on.

Then there was the problem of how to support people who were unable to earn a living and had no other means of support. Rentals were often paid but this still left the problem of how to cover incidental expenses. 'Thank you for your letter of the 4th inst,' he wrote on one occasion.

'We are paying 16/- per week for board and lodging of the family. In addition to this we shall have to find clothing and I have got Miss Mabel Cavan to see what is needed. She has very kindly promised to supply some of it herself. I think also that we ought to give the Belgian woman a little pocket money (say 2/- per week) as she is a very nice person and I do not like the idea of this class of Belgian having to come begging for every little thing they want. They naturally feel it as we should ourselves if we were in similar circumstances.'

The horror stories of atrocities continued to control the rumour mill, to such an extent that Mr Everest finally wrote to a colleague who had made enquiries as to the many mutilated Belgians said to be living in Shrewsbury – 'there are no cases of mutilation... I expect you have heard the rumour of the child with its hands cut off. This mythical child seems to be in every town in England.'

Reading through Mr Everest's file one can only be surprised that, in the circumstances, he had so few problems. But there was one family he was glad to see the back of – the Baacks.

'I had dreadful trouble with the Baacks yesterday. After we left them somebody seems to have told them a lot of fairy tales about Longden and they expected a place like they had in Belgium about five minutes from a big town. The son who is a Belgian officer came over last night and although he has been wounded and they have not seen him since the War began, the only welcome they gave the poor chap was a long tirade against you, me, Miss Hobman and Longden, and they would be glad if they could leave to-day. I told them they could do what they liked as we have done our best for them and if they are not satisfied we could not help it. The woman even said that the Germans were better than the English and she would go back to Belgium where apparently her husband has accepted employment under the Germans.'

The next correspondence is a copy of a telegram sent by Mr Everest telling the refugee committee at Earl's Court that the family was returning to London with the intention of going on to Belgium. There then follows another letter which reads:

'I cannot understand what the Baack family are doing with you again. When they left here they told me they were going to Paddington and would stop at a hotel and from there return to Belgium. They are not in need of money. As far as I could make out they have plenty. I found that they did not return to Paddington but to Euston.

'The son is a very nice fellow and I am very sorry for him. He had ten days or a fortnight leave to spend with his mother but he went off back to Leeds the next day.

'I hear from Aldwych that they are not to be re-allocated anywhere and I have taken steps to bring them to the notice of the Metropolitan Police and I think the woman from what she said to me wants watching very carefully. She certainly ought not be allowed to go back to Belgium.

'I do not think the Longden people will take another family. They have had such an unfortunate experience. Should they make me another offer I will let you know.'

One cannot help but sympathize with the son.

Of course, once the war was over most Belgians returned home. Some remained and perhaps the best known Belgian refugee to stay in England after the war was a certain Hercule Poirot, fictional though he may have been!

Chapter Five

The role of the King's Shropshire Light Infantry in the War

WHEN THE WAR broke out in August 1914 Britain's 'contemptible little army', as Kaiser Wilhelm II supposedly called it, didn't stand a chance. Despite its history of pressing men into the Royal Navy or the many stories of recruiting officers who sneakily put 'the king's shilling' in a tankard of ale and thus tricked men into the army, by the mid-1800s Britain's military was made up mainly of volunteers. Britain depended on a strong navy for its strength, not just within the British Isles but also within its Empire all around the world and, consequently, it was in those far-off lands that Britain's army was required to keep the peace. This meant that in 1914 Britain had only a small army of professional soldiers which didn't begin to compare, at least in size, with the conscripted armies of other European nations.

The numbers say it all. Britain then had less than 750,000 men in its army – of these some 200,000 were reservists who were suddenly called up and a further 247,000 were stationed abroad. This left less than 250,000 men to defend Belgium and France, not to mention Britain itself. The French government had, on the other hand, been preparing for a war against Germany for some years and so had a much larger army made up, mainly, of conscripted men: they had 823,000 men already serving with a further 2,870,000 reservists who immediately reported for duty. Meanwhile Germany, a country

Copthorne Barracks, Shrewsbury - Main entrance.
(David Benson)

Copthorne Barracks, Shrewsbury Library. *(David Benson)*

that like France had been preparing for war for years, had an army of over 4,000,000 altogether, also primarily conscripted men, whilst Austria-Hungary could call on upwards of 3,000,000 men.

Throughout the United Kingdom most regiments were initially associated with the counties within which they had first been formed. Shropshire was no exception with the King's Shropshire Light Infantry (KSLI) based in Shrewsbury. This regiment can trace its history back to the mid-1700s although as the county regiment of both Herefordshire and Shropshire it dates from only 1881.

Like many other such regiments the KSLI included within its forces many volunteers for home defence (in the unlikely event that this should ever be needed) who lived locally. As a Special Reserve volunteer a man was required to attend annual training for up to three weeks, during which time he would be paid five shillings and sixpence as a private and receive an allowance to cover expenses for his horse. Most men who joined as volunteers probably saw it as little more than an excuse for a summer break from their usual trades, a holiday almost, sometimes locally in places such as Oswestry or Walcot Park, sometimes further afield – in the Brecon Beacons, for example. Even the

The Maltings, Ditherington.

advertising for volunteers seemed to say as much. One advertisement in January 1914 enticingly described the provision of 'good pay, plenty of food, warm fires, cheery companions, football, boxing, billiards [and] reading room'. As it happened although the camps were usually held in May of each year, in 1914 it had been decided to postpone the camp until September by which time, of course, the war had begun and any volunteers on the books had been called up anyway.

The KSLI was mobilized on the day war broke out with its men billeted not just in Shrewsbury but also in Oswestry, Ludlow and Wellington. Within a fortnight some 6,000 soldiers had been drafted into Shrewsbury – over 1,000 men were based in the Maltings at Ditherington, others were in hotels around the town, the Music Hall, Shrewsbury School etc. (The reopening of the last for the autumn term, incidentally, was delayed by a week so that the place could be cleaned.) In the Quarry Gardens a large marquee was set up where the local branch of the YMCA could provide the men with reading and recreation areas and light refreshments. The *Chronicle* was delighted to report that 'the conduct of the soldiers has been exceptionally good' although there was a problem later for many of the officers who paid directly for their accommodation themselves but then forgot to ask for, or keep, any receipts!

Inevitably, with so many soldiers suddenly descending on the town, there were

Shrewsbury School.

concerns for the morals of the people of Shrewsbury. However, two years later the *Chronicle* was able to report that, despite the expectations of many moralists, the numbers of illegitimate births for 1915 showed a decrease of over 33 per cent compared with that of 1914!

Of course, in the first rush of people wanting to enlist, many Shropshire men wanted to join their Shropshire regiment. This wasn't always possible – it was then still a cavalry unit so those men who could not ride were rejected. They weren't the only ones rejected – one man refused to shave his beard but tried to recommend himself by saying he had

The Music Hall, now the Shrewsbury Museum and Art Gallery. *(David Benson)*

The Square in Shrewsbury; lining up to enlist. *(Shropshire Regimental Museum)*

'camped in Palestine'; another said he wanted to join the army 'but disliked killing anything'. In those early days of the war the selection boards still thought they could pick and choose! There were other problems too – country-bred Shropshire lads tended to be relatively healthy – and relatively large – so that finding uniforms to fit them was sometimes difficult. In fact, there were shortages of all types of equipment from weapons to bedding.

Not all local men automatically joined the KSLI. Historically, what had often happened was that regiments would traverse the country when recruiting, so that a regiment from the Scots Guards, for example, might find itself in Devon recruiting to the accompaniment of soldiers marching and bands playing. Impressionable young boys would see this and, years later when they were old enough to become soldiers themselves, would recall the buzz and excitement they had felt that day and would therefore feel that that particular regiment was the only one for them.

In the course of the war the KSLI, however, expanded to include twelve battalions, of which eight saw active service overseas. When war broke out some men were already serving abroad – the 2nd Battalion, for example, was in India at the time although by December of that year it had been moved to France. Similarly the 1st Battalion had been based in Tipperary and was also soon sent on to France. The 1-4th Battalion, on the other hand, was mobilized in Shrewsbury in August 1914 and then sent to serve first in

India and then in the Far East. Returning back to Britain after three years absence the men were sent, instead, directly to France in 1917 without even the chance to have a home leave. Another battalion that didn't initially go to France was the 10th Battalion – it was sent to Egypt to protect the Suez Canal from Turkish attack and subsequently saw action in Gaza and Palestine. It, too, however, ended up in France in 1918.

In Shrewsbury, a month or so after the war had been declared, there was a meeting in the Music Hall asking for volunteers for a Shrewsbury 'Pals' Brigade that was to be formed within the KSLI. A crowd assembled and 170 men immediately signed on. The colonel who addressed the meeting made what were by now the usual comments about how 'a man would fight better when he was in the company of his own pals'. Some, however, were concerned that this may cause the development of cliques within a unit but the colonel disregarded this, saying also that the army had no intention of letting such cliques develop and in fact, 'when the company had been out for a short time they would be a band of brothers'.

If der Shropshire Light Infantry haf gone by, den I kan kom out.

(Shropshire Regimental Museum)

In fact there was no true 'Pals' brigade within the KSLI as had been formed in many towns in northern England. However, the nearest equivalent within the KSLI could be said to be the 6th Battalion. By September 1914 this newly formed battalion left Shropshire for training and moved on to France in July of the following year. There followed over three years of service on the western front. This battalion alone was to lose 555 soldiers and twenty officers, not to mention the many hundreds that were wounded, gassed or taken prisoner.

Chapter Six

Letters Home

Letters from the Battlefield

Once war had broken out the desire for news of just what was happening in the different war zones became paramount. But, right from the start, any letters from the front were censored as was any news that appeared in the papers. Consequently, particularly in the first couple of years of the war, local papers up and down the country would often print letters that had been received by their readers. These too, of course, had been censored at source so that the editors of the various papers felt they could reprint them freely although they often added additional censorship by not giving the names of the people whose letters they were printing.

'Can't write often, I'm up to my neck in it.'

But despite all this, such letters give a fascinating picture of lives lived by men who would never normally have imagined finding themselves in such situations as they soon faced. The early letters tend to be unremittingly cheerful. One letter, written in September 1914 by Private Withers in the Transport Corps, begins,

'As you predicted it is not all beer and skittles, but it is better than it might have been. I have seen many exciting things, but nothing very alarming up to now has happened.

'It is very difficult to put much in a letter as we are not allowed to say where we are or where we have been; where we are going to we do not know. The organization of supplies is really wonderful, and great credit is due to those in authority. The German infantry are rotten shots, and all our men up to now have been killed by their

Germans lie dead as a result of attacking in massed ranks in the early part of the war. *(Taylor Library)*

artillery. The German losses have been enormous, and far exceed ours. They do not come one at a time, but ten deep… Of course we have retreated a considerable distance this week, but it has been done with an object in view.

'I have seen hundreds of aeroplanes, and saw a German one brought down by our artillery. There were four in it; one was alive when it landed. The places are full of German spies; it is quite a business shooting them.

'This war, I don't think, will last long.'

A month later Private Withers was still optimistic, writing to his father that:

'our men are fighting in the trenches six miles from here, while we can hear the boom of cannon all through the night… I saw 500 North African soldiers, absolutely black, today. Fancy meeting them in the dead of night… I still hold the same opinion that the war will not last long.'

A young man from Shropshire, Private Withers had probably never seen a coloured man before.

This ebullient mood survived for some time, at least in letters home which probably were deliberately cheerful. A letter received in the *Chronicle* offices in April 1915 was written by a rifleman in the Queen Victoria Rifles:

'You would not know our soldiers after a spell in the trenches, especially after having eleven days covered in mud and no shave or wash. We look like a band of tramps, except that we are happy and singing as we march along.'

British soldiers bailing out the trench. *(Taylor Library)*

The optimism of the soldiers in the early months of the war is astounding to us today knowing, as we do, what lay ahead. One letter written by a transport driver goes a little way to describe the mixture of boredom and duty felt by those men:

'I have charge of a 45 hp Leyland lorry, capable of carrying between three and four tons. I have another mate to help me. We have to keep the cars running, and take turn about in driving; and our military work consists of loading up the waggon at the nearest rail head with a specified kind of ammunition, taking same to the horse column, unloading into the horse waggons, which then take it on to the gunloaders and brigade reserves; but we have sometimes to take our waggons right up behind the big guns, when the horse columns are pushed. It is not really hard work, but the thing that palls most is the monotony of the whole business, as we are doing the same thing day after day. But it would not do to grumble, no matter how monotonous we feel things, as it is our duty; and we can help most in this terrible crisis by all doing out duty, and doing it cheerfully. We heard very little of how things are going further up in the line of battle; but judging by what we do hear, and read in the daily papers, of which we get a pretty good supply, and also by the quiet and peaceful appearance of the district we are in, we must be going on very well. I think the Germans by this time will know that the British Tommy is a terrible being once he is properly aroused. The Germans have gone the proper way about things to fairly rouse our men, by their ferocious and wanton behaviour in Belgium, and there can be no turning back until the power for a repetition of this terrible work is for ever taken out of their hands. Personally, I am standing the rigour of the campaign well, and feel in very good health, only, like everybody else, wearying to get home again.'

Not all the men who had joined the colours immediately war broke out found themselves so quickly at the front. Many spent months in other parts of Britain undergoing training which, judging by some of the letters, wasn't all beer and skittles either although there was still time for games:

'We have had a very busy week... we are doing such things as scouting, outposts, advancing under fire, digging and defending trenches etc... Most of us have got blisters on our hands from trench digging.

'This afternoon an XI out of our battalion played an XI out of the King's Royal Rifles. It was a draw 2-2. Two minutes from time we were leading 2-1 when one of their men hit the ball down with his hand, and scored for them. He had his back to the referee, so, of course, the referee did not see it – worse luck – as we particularly wanted to beat them, as they beat the Rifle Brigade 9-0 and they said they were going to beat us 20-0. I think we shall beat them next time, as we had one or two of our best men away, and they have played together before and our men have not.'

But most of the training was route marching and drill as described in another letter:

'We have had some pretty busy days this week although it rained all day Monday and Friday and we had to drill and attend lectures in the huts or in the wood. On

Tuesday and Thursday we started off about nine o'clock to a place about 7 miles away, where we had to cook our own dinners; then do some work, and march home again arriving about 7 o'clock. They gave us a meal for dinner, and some of us had a jolly sight better dinner than we get in camp, as we have had stew every day now for the last 11 weeks ... We are also doing a lot of bayonet exercises, as the bayonet has proved a very useful weapon in this war. I hope to be home for a day or two at Christmas, but we do not know anything definite yet.'

But it was when soldiers came home that a truer picture of conditions began to emerge and quite often these men then gave interviews to the *Chronicle*. One soldier home on leave told a reporter:

'It was a miserable time, wet day and night, and our men had to sleep out in the wet... This was where we started the big battle... [and] we managed bit by bit to climb the hill although the shells were flying at the rate of about

THOUGH YOU CAN'T SEE ME DEAR TO-DAY THIS LITTLE CARD IS SENT TO SHOW YOU WHERE I AM TO-NIGHT QUITE HAPPY AND CON"TENT"!

Post card from a training camp.

ten a minute all round us. When we got to the top we were practically surrounded by Germans, but our officer said we must not retire, we had to hold them. We were fighting all that day without a minute's rest bullets and shells were coming round us like hail. I have never seen anything so terrible. We harried them as much as we possibly could, and by night there were piles of German dead lying about in front of us. It was here we had experience of the white flag. The enemy showed the white flag, and when we went out to fetch our wounded we were met by a hail of lead, but we did not go back until we had brought 100 of them with us at the point of the bayonet. We were fighting hard for three days and three nights. Without any rest, at times up to our knees in water in the trenches... we were in and out of trenches for about 5 weeks, but nothing much occurred save a terrible shell fire every day, and an occasional infantry attack which was easily repulsed... We then went to Ypres and walked straight into the firing line. We were fighting all day on the 21st October and at night about 7.30, 250 of us crawled about half a mile to our left front and lay down in a field of turnips. We had scarcely got there when we saw a big blaze that appeared to come from a haystack, and we then heard some shouting and yelling and trumpets blowing and in a few minutes we saw thousands of Germans coming in masses. Our officer gave us the command

Awaiting the enemy. *(Taylor Library)*

to load up and fix bayonets. We lay in wait for them until they were within three or four hundred yards. They did not know we were there, and they came up in masses, singing and shouting. We opened into them with rapid fire, and I don't think there was one of them got back. After I had fired 10 rounds I was hit in the right hand, but I managed to get off another 20 rounds while my comrades must have got off about 50 rounds each into the solid mass of Germans. It appeared that every bullet took effect for they went down like nine-pins, leaving gaps in the masses as we fired. We lay for about three quarters of an hour watching the ground, but we did not see any movements – only heard groans. After that I had to retire to the hospital at the back of the firing line, and finally was invalided home. I rejoin at London next Saturday.'

Going to the trenches.

The men didn't necessarily have to come home for the true horror of the trenches to be revealed. A few lines from one letter written in October 1917, are particularly revealing:

'To the deuce with their bombs. I'd rather have shells, as they give you a sporting chance of getting out of their way. Every time our battalion go into the line we come back minus a few gallant lads, who have done their duty nobly. It's war and, well, it's hellish. One's thoughts often torment, but oh! it's hard to know of your fellow men being killed.'

As the war progressed there are fewer and fewer such letters and interviews. Instead, sadly, many of the letters quoted are letters of condolence from officers and men to the families of those who have recently died. Describing one soldier who had only joined up some two months before, his Commanding Officer wrote:

'As a "gentleman ranker" we all admired him very much and hoped to promote him and thus encourage him to apply for a commission. He was [hit with] other good fellows by a shell which fell in a courtyard of a farm in which the men were billeted and where I was paying out. Death was instantaneous as a piece of shell struck him on the head. His body was buried with every respect in a quiet little cemetery near by.'

This man's family was fortunate; they had the knowledge that his body had been buried

Wounded being transferred from a French hospital train to a hospital ship for transporting to 'Blighty'. *(Taylor Library)*

with due reverence. Not all families had that comfort. As a commanding officer wrote in another letter of condolence about another soldier:

> 'He was commanding a company on 28th March [1918] when the Germans made a very strong attack upon our lines. He was killed by a shell during the morning whilst in the trench with his company keeping them going under very intense shell fire. I feel his loss very deeply. I have always had the greatest admiration for his qualities and character, and he was also a most valuable officer and one that it will be impossible to replace. We were compelled to withdraw from the trench in which he was killed and so were unable to recover his body.'

Occasionally the letters give an indication of lighter or more amusing moments. One captain in the Shropshires was well known for 'the luridness of his language' and on returning from the trenches with his men he was approached by a staff officer he didn't recognize who hoped he and men would be able to secure good billets. 'I hope so,' the captain replied, 'they ---- well deserve them, for out of 88 days, we have been 68 in the trenches.' The captain later learnt that he had been speaking to the Prince of Wales.

Another soldier wrote home to describe how he had just been wounded:

> 'The bullet entered my left breast pocket, went through my wallet and pocket-book, and some letters. A sixpence, that Bert's sister gave me on Shrewsbury Station for luck, turned it (it is almost cut in two). It crossed my chest, just grazed my ribs, and came out at the bottom of my right breast pocket. I had a leather coat on, and it has blown about six inches out of it and my tunic. There would not have been much left of me if it had gone home, so I must think myself very lucky.'

Then there was the soldier describing how, when some German prisoners were captured, one of the prisoners spoke in excellent English saying 'Won't mother be pleased!' and another asked 'How long will it be before we are sent to England?' 'It is obvious,' the soldier remarked in his letter 'that the Germans are aware that prisoners of war have a 'cushy' time in England.'

One soldier, whose battalion had been mobilized in August 1914 and then sent to France, wrote a year later to a friend, 'one of our men picked up a white kitten while in Shrewsbury, and we still have it with us. It has been with us through all our wanderings, even in the trenches. Of course it is now very highly prized.'

The last word, though, must be that written by a soldier in a London hospital who wrote 'Dear Mother, This comes hoping it finds you as it leaves me at present. I have a broken leg, some shrapnel in my left arm, and dysentery...'

The War at Sea

Technically at least, soldiers fighting in the various battlefields around the world were supposed to be at least eighteen years old. There were no such restrictions for young lads joining the Royal Navy and boys of sixteen were often amongst the crews of the battleships.

One such sixteen-year-old midshipman was to write

Two Jacks.

home describing his experiences of the Battle of Jutland:

'I expect you will like to hear something about the action on the 31st [May 1916]. Well, the first thing we heard was that the enemy's Battle Fleet with cruisers and destroyers had been seen. That was about 3.30 in the afternoon. At 4pm we were told that the battle cruisers and light cruisers were engaging the enemy. Of course we increased to utmost speed to catch them up, and at about 5.30 we first heard the sound of firing away on our starboard bow. I was on deck all the time, ready to close up at any moment at the guns. At about 6pm we first sighted the battle cruisers, who had been in action some time. There were some protected cruisers with them. They were a mile or so ahead of us, and were firing jolly well, the enemy's shells were falling all round them, and by now I could see the flashes of the enemy's guns, although you could not see the ships themselves owing to the low visibility. Our cruisers were getting it hot, and we could see the enemy's shells hitting time after time, but they (the cruisers) still kept on firing splendidly. By 6.20pm all our ships ahead of us had got out of the way, and at 6.25pm we opened fire on the enemy's battleships. Of course their object was to evade an action with our Dreadnoughts, so they did a bunk, but we just managed to catch them, and we were firing for about half an hour intermittently. They must have had a nasty pommelling, as we were hitting right and left, but unfortunately we lost them about

Battleships of the British Grand Fleet in the North Sea as they head out to meet the German High Seas Fleet at Jutland.
(Taylor Library)

7pm, and then had to discontinue the action. I should think, taking into consideration the losses on both sides, that it was a drawn battle, but we did far more damage than they did, and they must have had many more casualties.

'I am afraid leave will be postponed for a month at least now, as the dock will be in use, but it can't be helped. If anybody at home is athirst for knowledge re the action, you must pass this assortment of bilge round, as I am incapable of another effort.

'PS I saw a Zepp. And was not impressed. Of course it is all rot that they inflicted any damage on any of our ships.'

That sixteen-year-old boy was quite right – although heralded as a victory by the press the Battle of Jutland can best be described as 'a draw' and for the rest of the war the German fleet was largely blockaded in its ports so that they were forced to change their tactics to using U-boats to attack ships mainly in the seas around Britain but also further afield.

One such attack took place in the Mediterranean in May 1917 when the SS *Transylvania* was torpedoed and sunk. Like the better known sinking of the RMS *Lusitania* in 1915 this was a Cunard passenger liner although, in this case, the ship was being used as a troopship. One person who lost his life was Guy Charles Dunlop Hill who 'gave his life to save others' and is remembered on a memorial in the church at Ford. Another Shrewsbury soldier, who survived, wrote a graphic account of the incident in a letter to his mother:

'I am just getting over the effects of being torpedoed... We were on parade on one of the upper decks of the transport, when suddenly someone pointed to a whitish-green streak moving at a fair speed in a direct line for us. Of course, the great majority instantly realized what it was. I instinctively clenched my teeth and fists and watched it, fascinated, during the brief seconds before the angle of the ship's side hid it from view. Then came a loud report, a trembling of the huge hull, and a deluge of water thrown up by the force of the explosion.

'There was no panic, but everyone seemed stunned by the suddenness of the thing. However, we were soon assured that the damage was not as serious as might have been expected, and the boats began to be lowered, whilst our two destroyer escorts came alongside, and soon moved off with crowded decks. Soon afterwards, however, we were struck again, and the ship began to have a decided list, so I made my way to the stern and got into a boat on the top deck; but just as we were about to be swung out preparatory to being lowered, I suddenly saw the bows of the ship begin to go down gradually; then a great wave of water seemed to come sweeping up the decks towards me. I remember hanging on for dear life as the stern of the ship came almost perpendicularly out of the water. Then down we went amidst the cracking and crashing of timber.

'My next experience was that of being drawn far down under the water, and I seemed to be the centre of a whirlpool, because I went down feet first, and all sorts of things seemed to be twisting round by body. Then I seemed to shoot up with alarming rapidity and come out on top again.

'Owing to my slight experience in swimming I was immediately in possession of my senses, and my first conscious act was to kick off one of my boots, the other having come off on its own (of course, I had previously unlaced them) and a few strokes brought me to an overturned boat, on to which I managed to pull myself. There must have been half a dozen of us on the same boat, and soon two more boats, also overturned, joined us as things will in the water... in about 20 minutes to half an hour after taking the water I found that all three overturned boats had drifted against the side of one of our destroyer escorts which was hove to waiting for us. We were all pulled aboard, and except for a severe wetting I was none the worse for my experience.

'A short time afterwards we were landed in one of the smaller Italian ports where we were received magnificently by the Italians, who seem to be the most kind hearted people I have come across. We stayed there a week, and are now back in ---- again refitting.'

Chapter Seven

Life goes on as Normal

DESPITE ALL THAT was happening in other parts of the world, for many people in England life went on very much as normal. There were fewer men around, of course, and everyone lived with the constant dread of the arrival of a certain telegram but, after all, farmers still had to tend their livestock, women still had to feed their children and those men who remained at home still had to go to work. People lived, and died, and were born, just as always. Spring followed winter and the weather was a subject of conversations as always. Some things never change.

But there were inevitable changes.

At times of war news becomes vitally important. It's difficult for us today to comprehend just what it must have been like – we are so used to news everywhere we go from the radio, the television and, now, the internet. Cinema was then still very much in its infancy and this applied particularly to newsreels, the making of which was hampered by the equipment required and the virtual impossibility of gaining access to sites where the action was taking place. Facts were what was wanted, as opposed to rumours which could start to spread so easily, something that with the internet we are once again becoming aware of. Indeed on one occasion the *Chronicle* had to publish a denial of rumours concerning the KSLI that had spread persistently in the town the previous week.

From the moment the war broke out the circulation figures of newspapers increased but there were problems here, too. As the war progressed paper came to be in short supply and, along with increasing costs in production and declining income from advertising, this caused many smaller newspapers to fold. By January 1918 the cost of

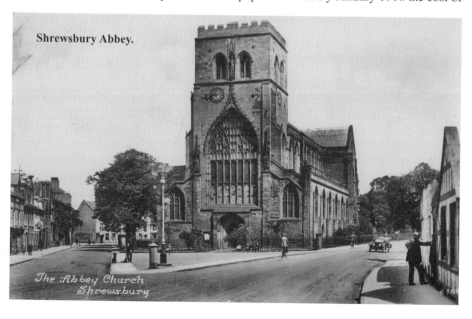

Shrewsbury Abbey.

The Abbey Church
Shrewsbury

Old Shrewsbury School, now Free Library.

Shrewsbury Library.

paper had risen 400 per cent from the time when the war began and more than 100 daily and nearly 700 weekly publications had had to increase their prices. The *Chronicle* managed to survive without increasing its price (one penny) but with fewer pages.

One way in which people could learn what was happening on the front was by attending lectures. The Abbey Foregate Literary Society was one group that gave regular lectures, usually in Shrewsbury School. And the society was able to command speakers of note, too. In February 1915, for example, Hilaire Belloc came to Shrewsbury to speak about the progress of the war and in March Sir Arthur Conan Doyle gave 'a graphic story of the four great battles' that had taken place up to that time. Other lectures included subjects like *What the British Navy is really doing*. In the autumn of that same year there was a talk titled *The German Spy System*, the speaker knowing 'more on this subject than any living Englishman' said the *Chronicle* when advertising the talk and went on to tell people that he would tell those who attended 'how efficient the German spy system has become and describe the many devices used by spies for obtaining information. Heady stuff.

Of course if you didn't want to spend your money buying newspapers or attending lectures, you could always visit the library and hope to find a paper that hadn't been defaced. Apparently at one time there was one regular reader who made a habit of scrawling the word 'Liar' on sections that didn't meet with his approval; he seemed to especially disapprove of one of the journalists who wrote for the *Daily Mail*.

Newspapers were not just purveyors of war news. They became leaders of opinion, mainly at this time encouraging strong anti-German sentiments amongst the populace. But they also served to inform the local community of what was going on in the area including any entertainments. And entertainment at such a time is extremely important, if only to boost the morale of the people at home.

Entertainment

Not all lectures were martial in tone. Subjects such as *Tramping and Canoeing in Central and South Africa* could well have made a pleasant change from reports of the war. For those of an erudite bent the activities of the Caradoc and Severn Valley Field Club also would have given a welcome release. This group continued with its meetings throughout the war and even, on occasion, managed to organize two/three-day trips to places like the Wye Valley or Nottingham, as well as more local visits within the county.

One curious series of 'Theosophical' lectures (not, in this case, arranged by the Caradoc and Severn Valley Field Club) were held in November 1914 and subjects included things like *The Other Side of Death.* This, however, gives an indication of how the war was, even then, already affecting religious beliefs during the war period. Whether or not religious belief increased at the time is debatable but, certainly, religious observance did. And in some not so usual forms, too. The more superstitious beliefs certainly increased as many people who had lost loved ones turned to spiritualists for succour or sought the help of fortune tellers. A number of fortune tellers in Shrewsbury were eventually brought to court and severely fined using a 1824 act against vagrants in an effort to stamp out the practice. There were regular predictions as to the future course of the war, invariably totally inaccurate as, for example, with one prediction in January 1915 that had been cast by so-called experts in Paris using a combination of coffee granules, magic mirrors and candle flames – they announced the war would end that coming February or March. Even the iniquitous habit of forcing people into sending chain letters whereby if the chain is broken bad luck will follow, a practice that today is to be found taking hold on the internet, was also undermining morale so that one Shrewsbury clergyman sent a letter to the *Chronicle* asking the paper to point out that such letters were mischievous and should be suppressed.

Inevitably though, just about all the usual types of leisure activities were affected by the war. Even as war was declared in August 1914 there were restrictions placed (some of them, to our minds, extremely petty) when Parliament passed the Defence of the Realm Act (DORA). This act was to give the government enormous powers allowing it to requisition buildings as required and control (or censor) newspapers; public clocks were not to chime between sunset and sunrise, whistling for a taxi and even the feeding of bread to wild animals became illegal. Pub opening times were limited and, in fact, all places of entertainment had to close by 10.30 pm. (Incidentally, along with the licensing laws another DORA law that survives to this day was the introduction of British Summer time in 1916.)

Even bank holidays were changed – in 1916 the Whit Monday Bank Holiday was postponed until August of that year. But despite such rulings, most people tried to carry on much as usual. In 1915 the *Chronicle* commented on the August Bank Holiday that despite dismal weather that drenched those people boating on the Severn, the 'hotels were filled to overflowing and all the resorts within easy distance [of the town] were also crowded out'.

Other events that drew the townspeople had for years included the annual Flower Show. This ceased to be held for the duration of the war but the gardens in the Quarry were still drawing people from far and near. One man from Wellington said that, having

The Shrewsbury Flower Show - notice the bandstand in the photograph which continued to be used during the war years.

never missed the Flower Show for many years, he decided to walk to Shrewsbury one summer's day just to see the Quarry Gardens as he considered it to be a 'flower show in itself'.

Perhaps while he was there he enjoyed listening to the band playing in the bandstand. Concerts were regularly given there during the summer months of the war although it has to be remarked that on one occasion there was an article in the *Chronicle* stating that 'We call attention to the fact that the Shrewsbury Borough Band includes in its programme music by Franz Lehar, an enemy composer who is in the field fighting against us'.

Babies continued to be born and, each year, the annual Shrewsbury Baby Show would be held in the Port Hill Gardens with a regular entry of some 200 babies each time. Older children were not forgotten with numerous events held for them and particularly for the children of serving soldiers in the various parishes of the town and they must have particularly enjoyed those occasions when the circus came to town.

The theatre was an important source of entertainment for young and old alike and there was a great range in the type of productions offered. Musical comedies and farces were very popular and, each year, pantomimes were produced. Variety shows were also popular with occasional troupes from overseas. Concerts were also given with the famous contralto, Miss Clara Butt, coming to Shrewsbury on several occasions. Many

THE INVINCIBLE TANK.

The Invincible Tank.

of Clara Butt's performances were given to raise money for war charities and in fact she raised somewhere between £30,000 and £40,000 altogether. As a result of this work she was later awarded a DBE (Dame Commander of the Order of the British Empire) in the 1920 civilian honours list.

The cinema was an increasingly important source of entertainment during these years and films by Charlie Chaplin are frequently found being advertised in the *Chronicle*. There was one film, however, that was not exactly a laugh a minute.

In 1916 the War Office decided to produce a film showing just what was happening on the western front. And so in August a film titled *The Battle of the Somme* went on public release. One hundred copies of the film were produced and within six weeks some 20 million people had been to see it; it was shown simultaneously in 20 cinemas within Birmingham alone and in many towns crowds coming to see the film were so dense that the police had to be called to control them. The film caused a sensation and, although there were some scenes in it that had been acted, by and large it was as accurate as the bulky cameras and difficult situation could make it.

That film never came to Shrewsbury but, some months later the War Office produced a second film on *The Battle of Ancre* which was shown in the town. There were three showings daily for the week it was there, with tickets costing from seven pence to one shilling and twopence. This film also showed the new tanks in operation.

War reporting had changed for ever.

Fund Raising

Throughout the war period so much of the entertainment in the town was really just an enjoyable means of raising funds for various war charities. In fact in the four years of

Fund-raising for the soldiers of the KSLI. *(Shropshire Regimental Museum)*

the war some 16,000 new charities were established in Great Britain and these ranged widely as regards the causes being supported from, at the beginning of the war, the Belgian refugees to the children of serving soldiers and, as the war progressed, to helping prisoners of war.

Right from the early days of the war Mrs Katherine Harley (whom I talk of elsewhere in the book) was busy raising funds for the supply of motor ambulances, for example. At first the sums raised seem somewhat pathetic to our modern eyes – a 'patriotic' concert is held in the Music Hall, for example, and the sum of £40 is given; a whist drive is held to provide comforts for the wounded in local hospitals at the end of which £8 is shared between three hospitals. Regular flag days were held and these tended to be much more successful with not just people standing in the street to collect but many women going from door to door. A Russian Flag Day in December 1915, for example, brought in over £300 – evidence that it was not just localized charities that were being supported.

As time went by, however, some ingenious methods of raising money were realized. Shops would advertise in the local paper that on a particular day a percentage of the profits would go towards the Red Cross or another designated charity. Concerts were held, children were encouraged to give up a treat so that the money saved could be donated to charity. In August 1918 a gymkhana was held to raise money for the KSLI

Prisoners of War Fund which raised (after expenses) over £700.

Sales would be held especially to raise funds and it's fascinating to see what was sometimes sold. In July the auctioneers, Hall Wateridge and Owen (which still trades in Shrewsbury although now simply as Halls) held an auction to which people donated items for sale. There were over 500 lots and the items included in the sale ranged from Worcester, Dresden and Coalport china, clarets and ports, books, even to dog kennels and puppies.

Other sales of unusual items were held regularly. A lamb was first taken for sale at Wellington market in June 1916; each time the animal was sold the buyer would then put it back into the market so that it could raise more money – by the time the sale(s) ended £400 had been raised. Similarly, a donkey was raffled on one occasion – I'm not too sure how the figures compute in this case because, according to the article in the *Chronicle*, some 1,099 tickets were sold raising £35 13s which does make one wonder just how much each ticket was sold for!

In another sale both 'live and dead stock' were sold; that sale in 1917 included a Pekinese dog which sold for £24. In yet another sale a pound of sausages was sold for £23 2s. The editor of the *Chronicle*, commenting on this sale, wondered how such news of the 'straits to which the English people are [obviously] reduced' would be received by the Huns.

It wasn't always money that was being sought, however. Not long after the war broke out an appeal was put in the paper asking for bicycles for the Shropshire Yeomanry because 'bicycles are of very great use in a mounted regiment for despatch riding, communication, and saving of horse-flesh in war. There are moreover in a mounted regiment a certain number of men for whom horses are not provided, and whose only recognized means of keeping up on the line of march is by walking. This in the case of

The Royal Salop Infirmary, now converted into apartments and shops.

a rapid or long march is not easy.' People were generous and a couple of weeks later the paper listed the names of all those who had donated bicycles to the regiment.

Even as they moved to the front there were requests for items to make life easier for the soldiers. As one soldier wrote 'I venture to appeal, through your columns, to any of your readers who may have old hockey sticks, balls etc for which they have no further use. We have scarcely any means of athletic recreation out here during the periods of rest out of the trenches, and I can assure you that any gift of sticks etc would be immensely appreciated.'

As the war progressed and the wounded came to Shrewsbury the local hospitals sought help, too. It comes as a shock to us today to realize just how little help was given to hospitals in the years before the establishment of a National Health Service. The Royal Salop Infirmary, for example, was already a well-established hospital serving people not just in Shrewsbury but throughout the county of Shropshire for many years. With its facilities stretched way beyond any previously envisaged limits it was soon in dire straits financially. By August 1916 the hospital had a debt in the region of £2,500 and was on the verge of financial collapse.

This debt translated into 50,000 shillings. And so a *Shilling Fund* was set up asking people throughout the county to give one or more shillings. Within a week of the appeal some 3,140 shillings had been raised and, by the end of that year they were more than half way to their target with over 33,000 shillings now in the bank.

It wasn't just the Royal Salop Infirmary that needed help either. Hospitals set up purely to cater for the war wounded were supplied only with medical essentials. The little things that made life easier for the men who were being treated were hardly top of the list of essential supplies. Things like gramophone records to entertain the soldiers or typewriters for use in the office. As the chaplain whose parish included the wounded in nearby Berrington Hospital pointed out in a letter to the *Chronicle*: 'On arrival in Blighty, the first thought of the men is to communicate with their relatives and friends, but they labour under the disadvantage of being very short of stationery, and gifts of paper and envelopes would be a very great boon. '

A few months later he was back again asking for help. He thanks the readers of the paper for the £27 6s they sent him and then goes on to say that 'all that money and a little more has now been spent upon cigarettes and notepaper. We badly need help for paper, soap, and cigarettes. During the last three months I have purchased out of the fund and distributed 50,000 cigarettes. This only means a packet of ten each man, once a week... To-night I had the pleasure of giving such a packet to 70 men fresh from Cambrai. I should like to ask [everyone to remember that when the soldiers] go into a hospital somebody has to find them in cigarettes.'

Finally, when the war ended, the same gentleman wrote once again thanking everyone who had helped his cause. Altogether he had received over £200 from local people.

Not all fund-raising, however, was for charity. The Government needed additional cash too and so decided to sell War Bonds. In August 1914 the gold reserves of the Bank of England and all banking institutions in Great Britain amounted to around £9 million. In those days the August Bank Holiday was held at the beginning of August and so, with the declaration of the war on 4 August, David Lloyd George, who was then Chancellor,

French postcard encouraging people to save rather than spend.

extended the holiday in order to allow time for the Government to pass a Currency and Bank Notes Act. Such control was essential to avoid any possibility of a run on the bank and also it meant that later on it was easier to control inflation.

The first War Loan was issued in the following November. Basically this was a loan

Sopwith Camel with advertising for War Bonds on the side. *(RAF Shawbury)*

that ordinary people could give to the country at a guaranteed rate of interest (in this case 3.5 per cent) to be paid back in the latter 1920s. Later War Loans were issued at varying rates of interest as the war progressed, accompanied with advertisements to encourage people to buy. 'Lend your money to the country,' said one advertisement, 'The soldier does not grudge offering his life to his country. He offers it freely, for his life may be the price of Victory. But Victory cannot be won without money as well as men, and your money is needed. Unlike the soldier, the investor runs no risk.'

Bearing in mind the comparatively small size of the local population, the people of Shropshire paid in enormous sums of money and these are regularly noted in the local papers. To make it easier for people to purchase war bonds, in January 1918 they became available for sale in post offices – pay down £5 and take away a bond. This issue of bonds guaranteed five shillings interest per annum followed by a return of £5 5s in 1927. Then in March, by which time many people must have already bought numerous bonds, a new War Loan campaign began and Salopians were asked to contribute some £75,000, an average (it was estimated in the *Chronicle*) of £2 10s per head. They bought £230,810 worth of bonds!

Crashed Sopwith Camel - notice all the children along with the adults in the picture. *(RAF Shawbury)*

Christmas

Most of us have heard the stories of the Christmas truce that took place along many sections of the western front battlefield on Christmas Day of 1914. The football games and exchange of cigarettes and war souvenirs, the sharing of photographs and, in a number of cases, it was an opportunity for German soldiers to write brief letters to girlfriends in England and get the British soldiers to post them.

At home things were less dramatic but people did their best to make a brave showing, if only for the children in their families. One effect of the war was to make goods that had to be imported much scarcer. Germany had for many years been a major producer of toys and had found a ready market for these in Britain – this, naturally, came to an end once war broke out and it was to be some years before much effort was made at home to bridge the gap in this market.

(Shropshire Regimental Museum)

These days we tend to think of turkeys as being mass produced in Norfolk but, although there was already some home production of turkeys, many were imported from Serbia, Hungary and even Russia at that time. One announcement in the *Chronicle* in November 1914 warned that there was therefore likely to be a scarcity of turkeys that year but, on the other hand, there were plenty of geese so that 'the rearer of geese will have a more than usually profitable season'.

By Christmas of 1915 the war had become almost an everyday fact of life. All those whose sons, husbands, fathers were away fighting had become used to writing regular letters so that getting in touch and sending gifts at Christmas became an important part of the annual festivities. It is interesting to note the regularity with which letters could be sent and received, particularly by those on the western front. Mail took only a couple of days to get from towns and villages in England to the trenches and it was quite the norm for people to send freshly baked cakes or even flowers on occasion to their loved ones. Indeed many shops had long since realized the importance of this potential market, offering to supply all manner of essentials for the soldiers. There were advertisements in the papers reminding people of the requirements of the soldiers; and not just foodstuffs but, for example, tins of lice powder: 'Kill that insect, Tommy,' ran the advertisements, 'When you haven't time to wash, there's a big chance you'll have "little companions". A little Harrison's Pomade kills every insect on hair and body.' I'm sure the men wished it could have been that easy.

Consequently, as Christmas approached appeals would be sent out for gifts for those soldiers who didn't regularly receive items from their families or there would be reminders as to the last posting dates to ensure prompt arrival. Parcels for the western front had to be despatched by 13 December, letters by 17 December. The Post Office also reminded people that all parcels had to be 'completely and fully addressed, with the name and address of the sender on the outside, and securely and strongly packed in covers of canvas, linen or other strong material'. Despite the Post Office insisting that there should be no fresh fruit or bottles within the parcels, this didn't stop requests for donations of just such things along with eggs, hams, chocolates, biscuits and cigarettes by people who were filling hampers to be sent to hospitals not just in France but also in places like Malta and Egypt.

Quarry Place Hospital. *(David Benson)*

Back in England people tried to carry on much as normal. But things weren't the same. At the end of 1916 the *Chronicle* commented that 'railway men probably never remember such a quiet Christmas as the one just past. The general public were not travelling much... Practically the only time when the accommodation was uncomfortably congested was on Christmas Eve, when many soldiers and munition workers were travelling'. Furthermore, 'many people this year forebore to send Christmas messages, and as a result postal servants, despite a depleted staff, managed very comfortably'.

The focus at home throughout the war years was very much on making the festive season as joyous as possible for those wounded and in hospital. The hospital staff went to a deal of trouble to decorate wards and enliven the atmosphere; at the hospital in Quarry Place, for example, all the soldiers woke on Christmas morning to find stockings at the end of their beds. There were concerts and carol singing and the local gentry came visiting and bearing gifts.

The children of serving soldiers were not forgotten either with parties being arranged for them in church halls. It will have been hard for the children who were only too aware of the scarcity of essentials. One poignant tale that reminds us of this was described in the *Chronicle* in December 1917 when one young girl was allowed by her mother to empty her money box a few days before Christmas. She left the house with her hands full of coppers and the mother imagined that the child had gone to spend her savings on toys and sweets. An hour later the girl returned home, not laden with toys but dragging a truck which contained 1cwt of coal, her Christmas present for her mother.

Many people visit family churchyards at Christmas time, leaving holly wreaths behind on the graves of loved ones. That Christmas of 1917 the *Chronicle* noted that such wreaths 'this year were more numerous than ever'.

However, the mood by Christmas 1918 had at last changed so that the Editor was then able to write: 'For the first time for four years, we feel that we can wish our readers a Happy Christmas... When we sit in the view of the Yule log blaze, there may be vacant chairs in the circle; all on earth that remains of those who filled them before the enemy unsheathed the sword is mingling with the soil of France or Belgium; but the little mounds that cover them are the footprints of the men who went to fight for the cause of that peace and justice... That fact should be a balm of healing to wounded hearts... Feeling this, and believing it, we hope there will be a measure of real happiness this Christmastide.'

Yours faithfully, Disgusted of Shrewsbury

Letters to the local press often give a fair indication of just how people in the community are thinking and those printed in the *Chronicle* are probably typical of many throughout the country in the war years. Within days of war being declared DORA was passed in Parliament and in one of the major measures covered by this act the government gave itself powers to censor anything printed in the press. Thus, it immediately became an offence to print anything that could be deemed to prejudice recruiting into the armed forces or cause any disaffection within the public at large; inevitably, too, what the press could say about military matters and the way the war was being run was strictly controlled.

Local newspapers often got around these measures by printing letters sent from the front to people in the community – after all such letters had, presumably, already been passed by censors. Such letters are fascinating but equally interesting are those letters that remind us of the situation at home, particularly letters of complaint about how people at home were reacting to or even ignoring the very fact that the country was at war. 'Disgusted of Shrewsbury' was alive and well and only too ready to complain.

One such letter was printed in May of 1916 and the writer complained that 'I have often heard it suggested that Shrewsbury is one hundred years behind the times, and judging by local happenings it will be something approaching a century hence before some of our civic fathers realize that this country is now engaged in a life and death struggle. We hear much about the urgent necessity for economy and the national need for the increased cultivation of land. On Tuesday therefore, when I saw men engaged digging up the turf of the lawn in front of the Shrewsbury Free Library I jumped to the conclusion that the Corporation were setting the public a good example by converting the lawn into a vegetable garden. I was surprised to learn, however, that it was flower beds that were being made. When the work is completed and the flowers are in bloom, I would suggest that a photograph is taken of the spot, and copies sent to all the Shropshire boys at the front. Such a charming reminder of how Shrewsbury is doing its bit could not fail to cheer them up and intensify their fighting spirit!'

Signed 'No Flowers' this letter produced a barrage of correspondence both for and against with one writer taking the opportunity to state that Shrewsbury was certainly not 'one hundred years behind the time' and used his letter to whine about the decadence of modern Sundays with 'sweet shops open for the boys and girls to patronize, tennis and

Flowers of a different kind were to colour the garden in front of the library in 1919.
(David Benson)

cricket in full swing before the open gaze of the public, all with open and flagrant disregard of the day of the Maker of it. For those who prefer something quiet there is the Sunday paper, and we see dignitaries of the church, ministers, and other professedly devout people eagerly buying them, and carrying them in a conspicuous manner as an example of modern Sabbath keeping. Then, sir, those of us who prefer the old paths, and attend places of worship, lest by chance we should forget the times in which we live, are very often forcibly reminded of military matters by the rousing strains of martial music poured forth by a band whose chief aim apparently is to make as much noise as possible, more especially when in the immediate neighbourhood of a House of Prayer'. In the end the editor was forced to inform his readership that this subject of correspondence was now closed.

Many people used letters to complain about behaviour. There is seldom any indication of who the complainant is nor exactly whom he's complaining about as in one letter written in 1917 where the writer is taking a dig at an officer who was evidently very self-conscious of the importance of his rank. 'Who,' the writer asked, 'was the important Major who recently in the street addressed a Subaltern... back on leave after 17 months service in France and Belgium, and enquired in imperious tones if he was aware of the new order requiring him to salute Home Service Officers of higher rank?'

But not all the letters are so pompous with some letters being sent by people wondering how they, 'too old at 45', in one case, can help the war effort or giving suggestions as to how paper could be collected ready for reuse rather than just being burnt.

Then, too, there are the poignant letters in which people are asking for information about loved ones lost on the front. One such letter, printed in April 1916, was particularly moving. It was sent by a gentleman who lived in Burnley:

'Sir, On Jan 22nd my son was killed in France after rescuing a wounded soldier who was helpless; he went and fetched him in under heavy machine gun and rifle firing from the enemy. My son brought the wounded comrade into the trenches all right, and was in the act of climbing the parapet to get into the trenches himself when he was shot and killed right away. I have just heard from his comrades that the wounded soldier is in hospital somewhere in England, and I should very much like to know where he is as I should like to get in communication with either him or his relatives. His name is Lance-Corporal Evans, and his home is somewhere in Shrewsbury, so I am given to understand, and my late son and Evans were stationed in Shrewsbury before going out as they were in the Shropshire Light Infantry. I would visit Evans if he is in hospital anywhere near here, as there are a lot of wounded soldiers in a hospital close to, and it would cheer him up a bit if we went to see him. I have made a lot of enquiries all over the place, but I cannot get any further information. I have been advised to write to you to see if you could through your paper get me any information. Thanking you for your trouble. I remain, yours truly, George Manders'

Mr Manders did find Lance Corporal Evans; he was in hospital in Halifax having had both his legs amputated. Manders' son, who had saved his life, was only sixteen years of age.

Sport

One of the first things to be affected by the outbreak of war is often sporting fixtures despite the fact that sport can be a great morale booster. One obvious explanation for this, of course, is that it is young men primarily who partake of sports and it is those same young men who are the first to enlist. This was definitely true in 1914 although it was the amateurs rather than the professionals who joined up first.

Football, then as now, was the most popular of all spectator sports. January 1914 opened with the first round of the English Cup when 32 matches were played around the region with, according to the *Chronicle*, '541,000 people attending giving cash receipts totalling £19,504'. That season Shrewsbury just failed to come at the top of the Birmingham and District League (being beaten at the end by Worcester). With a war only expected to last 'until Christmas' there seemed no reason in August to automatically abandon the fixtures for the coming season. By December, however, attitudes were changing and there was general disgust at the fact that a large number of professional players seemed to be holding back from enlisting. In January 1915 *Punch* magazine went so far as to refer to the football results as *The Shirkers' War News*.

This is exemplified in a letter that appears in the *Chronicle* in December in which the writer states, 'Now that the London newspapers have decided upon not giving details of professional football matches (only results), I think it is time for the country papers to shew themselves equally patriotic. There are many thousands of volunteers coming from the other side of the world (many at great sacrifice) to fight for the Empire. What must be their disgust to find that the very fittest men in Old England have decided to play football, instead of rallying round the flag? Well may the Germans think us a decadent race when such a state of things is allowed.'

This recommendation wasn't immediately followed by the paper which, in its next issue, reported that that week's game had been played 'before nearly 2,000 spectators, including 748 soldiers'. So that was alright then.

Then in the months that followed, as wounded soldiers started to be brought home, special arrangements were often made for them to attend the match as in a report that appeared in March 1915 which mentioned that 'a large number of wounded soldiers were present at the Villa match at Shrewsbury on Saturday, by the kind invitation of the Town committee'.

But that season was to see the end of the League until after the war. Football did continue, but in the guise of charity matches with teams regularly coming from Shrewsbury School, the railway workers or men from the Army Pay Corps for example, the charities being supported ranging from the Red Cross to the local hospitals.

Towards the end of the war people were obviously beginning to look forward with greater confidence once again so that, even before the Armistice, plans were being made to reintroduce the annual Christmas-time match between Shrewsbury and Wellington. Initially it was planned as a fund-raising match for the KSLI Prisoners of War Fund but by the time the match was played, on Boxing Day, that had been changed so that instead it supported a KSLI Disabled Prisoners of War Fund.

It wasn't just at home that Shropshire men were playing football. One letter from the western front gives a delightful picture of a match played there:

'Thanks for letter, parcel and papers, but the post has been rather erratic lately owing to mines or something in the Channel. I have sent you a few souvenirs – German and English cartridges, pieces of shell, a ring I made of two German shrapnel bullets, and knives used by the Gurkas. There is a football match on this afternoon. There was some difficulty at first in securing short trousers; but they have solved the difficulty by buying 11 ladies' blue --- [whatever word the writer used has been deliberately blanked out by the paper!], with little bows at the knees. I expect they will remove the bows for the fray.'

Many sports did continue through the war years to a greater or lesser degree. Being a rural county hunting, shooting and fishing interests were paramount. Interestingly, many working in this industry were given exemption when it came to enlistment – the continued breeding of quality horses to work on the front was too important – so that hunting largely continued although the season was shortened.

One young man ended up in court when he tried to sell a pheasant he had 'accidentally shot when shooting crows' and was fined ten shillings. The judge told him he would be 'better shooting Germans instead of pheasants'. And appeals regularly appear in the paper asking, when pigeons are being shot, if they can be sent to the hospitals to augment their rations. It wasn't just pigeons that were sought either – one letter in the paper asked that local people who had convalescent soldiers staying with them should get in touch so that any game shot that season (the winter of 1914) could be distributed to them.

The Pengwern Boat Club, then as now, played an important part in Shrewsbury's sporting fixtures. During the war years these inevitably decreased. However the Boat Club did its best for the war effort by regularly taking wounded soldiers for outings on the river. One delightfully worded article in the *Chronicle* describes how 'the journey occupied about two hours and on return to the club house the maimed warriors were entertained to a "smoker" in the course of which refreshments and smokes were supplied to them. A thoroughly enjoyable time was spent, and the Tommies were enthusiastic in expressing their gratitude for all that had been done for them.'

The Pengwern Boat Club.

One unusual sport that came to Shrewsbury was baseball. It was more of a demonstration match with two teams (one Canadian and one American) travelling around the country playing games, very much as a public relations event. They came to Shrewsbury in September 1918 and played at the Gay Meadow somewhat to the bemusement of the locals who 'found it a difficult matter to appreciate the points of the game'. Judging by the comments quoted in the *Chronicle*, however, the game was obviously much enjoyed by those from the other side of the Atlantic who were based in the area and shouted to the players things like 'No need to aim it. You couldn't hit a balloon' or, when one player after failing to hit a ball began to examine his bat, 'There's nothing wrong with the bat – it's the batter'.

Some things never change, whatever the sport that is being played.

Chapter Eight

Women at Home

THE 1914-18 WAR totally changed the lives of women for all time. More women, of all classes, now entered the working world and the kind of work they did changed, too. Before the war the most common form of employment for women had been domestic service which, the 1911 census showed, employed some 1.6 million women, roughly a quarter of the female workforce. Mind you, that same census return also showed the remarkable range of work that some women did – teaching was an obvious profession for women and here they outnumbered men by more than two to one. But women were working in such diverse jobs as photographers, blacksmiths, shipwrights, plumbers, pilots on barges and there was even one cab-driver.

This change in attitude by women themselves was therefore already taking place long before the war started. It was the Suffragette Movement that, more than anything else, brought it to the notice of the general public. In the months leading up to the war there were two subjects that constantly featured in the press of the time – the suffragettes and the situation in Ireland. One (to us, today, amusing) article appeared in January 1914 in the *Chronicle* commenting on the recent enfranchisement of women in Iceland 'at the comfortable age of forty. This may appear a somewhat advanced age of discretion, and certainly the woman who cannot use a vote by the time she is forty is hardly to be trusted with the complicated administration of a household.'

The subject was still argued against, and not just by men either. There were regular lectures held in Shrewsbury's Music Hall by the Church League for Women's Suffrage

The theatre in the Music Hall.

for the cause and a glance through those early papers shows that there are just as many lectures held in the same venue in opposition. The declaration of war in 1914 brought about a truce between the two factions, however, when people gathered together to support their fighting men.

Many charities were established and, to begin with, women set about sewing and knitting to supply the men with spare shorts, pyjamas, socks... As a *Chronicle* article pointed out 'the Shropshires at the front could do with a supply of socks. It is pointed out that it is a great comfort to the men to have a dry change on coming out of the trenches. We feel certain that we have only to mention this fact to stimulate the many who are working for the soldiers to pay special attention to the needs of the lads from round the Wrekin.' It wasn't long before everyone was knitting although not all the socks were gratefully received. As one soldier was later to remark 'some of the efforts that arrive are very thin and shoddy. Especially do I condemn the atrocity known as the heelless sock'.

A PAIR OF SOCKS

The women weren't just knitting socks, however. Clerical work soon proved to be very popular. Courses were advertised training girls in shorthand, typing and book-keeping and, in Shrewsbury, a number of girls went to work in the Army Pay Offices. This led one gentleman to write a stinking letter to the paper complaining at the horrendous rates of pay the girls were receiving: 'Sir, The Army Pay Offices and the Records Office are unnecessarily extravagant in the rate of the wages paid to young female employees. In Shrewsbury, quite young girls, only just 16 years of age, with no experience whatever, and who have not long left Elementary Schools, have been taken on as clerks at a commencing salary of £1 a week. I submit that this is far too high a wage for young inexperienced girls... These girls would have thought themselves well paid if offered ten shillings a week to commence.'

Other jobs, however, didn't receive quite the same remuneration and many were done quite voluntarily. There were a number of groups of women who would meet regularly to prepare swabs, bandages, splints and so on for the British Red Cross. One such group in the nearby village of Hodnet in one year made 276 pairs of ward and surgical shoes, 192 knitted face washers, 59 pairs woollen socks, 190 comfort bags, 35 surgical pads and 7 pairs of woollen mittens. One particularly unusual volunteer group met at the Conservative Club in Wem to prepare sphagnum moss for use as dressings in local hospitals; before long they were also supplying two hospitals in France as well. Another odd task, this time undertaken in Shrewsbury, was the production of hay nets for horses and mules at the front – these women even got a War Office contract to supply 20,000 of the nets (with, later on,

Edgmond Agricultural College. *(The Francis Frith Collection)*

another order for 36,000) and the women who were producing them earned 'good money'. Another group was busy preparing sandbags to be delivered to the front.

With the departure of so many men it was not long before women were taking on jobs previously undertaken by men. Women were soon working as sorters at the Post Office; 'strong' women were required at the Ditherington Maltings or to work as chauffeurs; many women who had retired from the teaching profession once they married were called back to replace the men who had gone. It was even suggested at one point that women could be called on to serve on juries at inquests but nothing ever came of that idea.

There were certain trades from which, no matter what tempting pay and conditions there may be elsewhere, women could not leave – these included those working in metal trades, pottery and glass manufacture, chemical trades, the leather industry and the like. In Shropshire, being a rural county, much of the work that was available for women was necessarily agricultural and there was soon a desperate need for women to replace the men who had been called up. In 1915 a special course of two weeks training was given at the Harper-Adams Agricultural College. It was such a success that the following year the training was extended to a month, and grants were given so that women who applied for the course had all their expenses paid. Not all the farmers were happy about this labour force 'lilac sunbonnet brigade' as some termed it, but it was very much a case of like it or lump it and, really, they had no choice. In fact the Women's Land Army (which was formed in 1917) proved to be very successful and without it many would have starved. By mid-1918 there were well over 100,000 women serving in this way.

How much difference the role of women behind the scenes in the First World War made to the suffragette movement is debatable. Undoubtedly, women would have soon been given the vote regardless but, whatever the effect of their war work, finally, in the election that followed soon after the war ended, women aged 30 and over had their chance to vote.

And the Children Helped too

Children who lived on farms had always helped with the work. In rural communities, too, it had long been the custom that schools would close so that all the children could help bring in the harvest. But the war changed their lives too. No sooner had war been declared in August 1914 than Lord Harlech, as Chief Scout, reminded Scouts up and down the country of their duty to help in all ways.

At first, as with their mothers, the children (or at least the girls) started to sew and knit. In February 1915 the *Chronicle* quotes a letter from a soldier to a schoolgirl at Wyle Cop thanking her for her parcel of socks: they 'were very much appreciated by the men who were fortunate enough to receive them, as they are comforts which are most useful. Although not a Shrewsbury man myself, I have lived in the county all my life, and I am very pleased to find that the Shropshire people, both young and old, are trying to do their best to assist Tommy to fight not only the Germans, but this bitter weather.'

With the harvest, as ever, children throughout the county turned out to help. And it wasn't just the standard crops either – in September 1917 the government issued a request for horse chestnuts to be collected by children and teachers and sent in baskets and sacks to the Director of Propellant Supplies. Why horse chestnuts?

The public was never actually told just what they were needed for in case word would get to the Germans of how they were being used. Apparently, in the years leading up to the war, cordite used in the munitions industry required wood for its production. The wood used was mainly birch, beech or maple and much of it was imported from North America. Once war broke out not only was this import seriously impeded but it was impossible to get enough of the stuff and so experiments were made to find another material as a substitute. Grain and potatoes worked but were needed to feed a population on the brink of starvation. Eventually it was discovered that 'conkers' could serve as a substitute.

Up and down the country children set to the task of collecting them. In fact they were so successful that there weren't enough trains to transport them to their destination (a factory at King's Lynn, Norfolk) and piles of them were later to be seen rotting at railway stations.

Two boys in Shropshire, however, found themselves in a spot of bother when they tried to help. On their way home from school one day, William Price went along a piece of waste ground where there were some chestnut trees. He and another boy threw sticks at the conkers because, as they explained later, their school teachers had asked them to obtain as many conkers as possible for the war effort. The maid at the house to which the ground was attached, Broome Hall, ran after young William and pulled him through the ditch into the Hall's grounds.

The house was then occupied by Belgian refugees, Mr and Mrs Nieuwenhove, and at this point Mrs Nieuwenhove arrived on the scene to help the maid. Soon afterwards Mr Nieuwenhove turned up, grabbed William and took him and locked him in their cellar.

Meanwhile William's friend had run away to raise the alarm so that then William's mother arrived and demanded that her son should be returned to her. Mr Nieuwenhove wanted Mrs Price to fetch the police, but she told him she only wanted her boy. Mr

Nieuwenhove then went into the cellar to fetch the boy only to find that William had escaped through a window.

Mrs Price complained to the police so that Mr and Mrs Neiuwenhove, along with their maid, ended up in court accused to wrongful arrest. In court William and his friend explained what they had been doing. At this point Thomas Ashby, assistant master at St Michael's Street Council School, said he saw the maid pulling the boy along the path in the direction of Broome Hall grounds. He admitted that the schoolboys had been asked to get as many conkers as possible, but he could not say that they had been warned not to trespass. This caused the barrister for Mr and Mrs Nieuwenhove to remark that it was absurd that boys should be let loose on people's property by order of their schoolmasters.

It was at this point that the judge stopped the case. He agreed that Mr and Mrs Nieuwenhove had suffered a great deal of annoyance by trespass at Broome Hall and it was perhaps unfortunate that they put the little fellow in the cellar, but in the circumstances he could not see his way to convict, and the case would be dismissed. The end result was that Mr and Mrs Nieuwenhove left the court complaining that, according to Belgian law, they would have been amply justified in placing the boy in the cellar, and his parents would have rejoiced that he had been so punished.

Conkers notwithstanding, other products were urgently needed for harvesting. And not just at harvest time either. It was suggested that youngsters in the area could make themselves useful retrieving the tufts of wool left on bushes by nearby sheep. These, once cleaned, could be used for making blankets.

Older boys, however, would be much more useful and schools in the town advertised the services of their boys on Saturdays. Writing in the *Chronicle* a master at the Lancasterian School said that he had 'upwards of 30 lads willing and anxious to help on farms on Saturdays. About a half have bicycles. The others therefore will be available for farms only in the immediate neighbourhood of the Borough unless farmers are willing to fetch them and bring them back in the evening'.

By May 1918 the labour shortage had become so critical that the Minister of National Service, A.C. Geddes, wrote an open letter to newspapers around the country stating that 'the military situation has necessitated calling up a large number of agricultural labourers, which will seriously deplete the available labour during the coming hay, corn and potato harvests. It is of vital importance that the harvest of these crops should be successfully secured this year. This success will depend largely upon boys at public and secondary schools, who

BLESS HIS LITTLE HEART! HE'LL MAKE A KITCHENER SOMEDAY

have reached an age that will enable them to do useful work on the land.

'The extent to which farmers are counting on their help is shown by the fact that demands for over 17,000 boys have already been received at this Ministry; and there is no doubt that this number will be largely increased when the full effect of the calling up for military service has been appreciated by the farmers. Of this number, not less than 3,000 will be required during June and July, and a further 3,000 are needed for October for potato lifting if suitable accommodation can be arranged.

'In view of the above facts, I am reluctantly compelled to appeal to schools to release, during term time, such groups of boys as may be necessary for getting in the harvest. This is a time of national crisis and the ordinary considerations of education have not the same force as in normal times. As I have pointed out, it is necessary to provide men for the army, and it is necessary to provide labour to take their places on the farms, and I must urgently appeal to parents, headmasters and boys to give all the help they can....'

Feeding the country's children had become more important than educating them.

Chapter Nine

Women at War

NOT ALL WOMEN were content to sit at home and knit socks (whether with heels or without) for the troops. Some even went to the front.

One such was Katherine Harley. Katherine Mary French was born in May 1855. Her father, William French, was a naval officer but, by the time she was ten years old, he had died and her mother had been committed to an asylum. Katherine was then raised by relatives.

Her elder brother, John, initially joined the navy but subsequently transferred to the army. He had a distinguished career serving in Sudan and the Boer War and, when war broke out in 1914, he was placed in charge of the British Expeditionary Force in France. He was replaced in this position in December 1915 by Douglas Haig and then served as Commander of the British Home Forces until the end of the war. Meanwhile Katherine had married Colonel George Harley but had been widowed when he was killed in the Boer War.

When war broke out in 1914 Mrs Harley initially decided to support the war effort by raising funds to supply a motor ambulance to go to France. Such fund raising was very popular and, looking back one hundred years, it is somewhat poignant to know that the initial response to her efforts was a letter from the British Red Cross Society which thanked her for her 'generous offer of a motor ambulance. As a matter of fact,' the letter went on to say, 'the appeal in *The Times* for motor cars has been so successful that we have had reason to close it...'

Mrs Harley was not to be so easily discouraged. A week later the *Chronicle* (20 November 1914) wrote 'Mrs P.D. Harley, of Condover Grange, feels sure that all those ladies who have so generously contrived towards the Motor Coffee Stall, will be glad to hear that the chassis is bought, and that the coach builders undertake to put the body on in a fortnight, so that in less than three weeks it should be

Katherine Harley; notice that she is wearing the Croix de Guerre awarded to her by the French government.
(Churches Conservation Trust, St Mary's, Shrewsbury)

ready to start for the Front.' Another week passed and she was in touch with the newspaper once again to say that she still needed a further £50 to make up the £800 required. This request was followed in the paper by a listing of all those who had already contributed – the list extends to two columns of print, nearly 18 inches in length!

A few months later Mrs Harley sent her apologies to the Atcham Board of Guardians, of which she was a member, to say that she was unable to attend as she was off to serve with the Scottish Women's Hospital at Royaumont in France as their financial administrator.

The Scottish Women's Hospital was founded in 1914 with support from the National Union of Women's Suffrage Societies and the American Red Cross. Its founder, Dr Elsie Maud Inglis, initially offered her services to the War Office; her intention was that they should perhaps serve alongside the Royal Army Medical Corps or other official medical units. The authorities, however, thought differently and one of them actually told Dr Inglis, 'My good lady, go home and sit still.' So she set up her hospital under the auspices of the French Red Cross instead. By the end of the war the Scottish Women's Hospitals managed 14 medical units, not just in France but also in Corsica, Malta, Romania, Russia, Salonika and Serbia, providing nurses, doctors, ambulance drivers, cooks, orderlies... One Serbian official who saw what the women achieved said of them, 'It is extraordinary how these women endure hardship; they refuse help and carry the wounded themselves. They work like navvies. No wonder England is a great country if the women are like that.'

On her arrival in France with the Scottish Women's Hospital Katherine Harley was put in charge of the administration of what was known as Auxiliary Hospital 301 at Royaumont – a 200 bed hospital in a thirteenth century abbey. Everything that was needed in the hospital had to be brought from England and there were constant problems. For example at one time ten beds were lost for several months – it was later discovered they had been filched by another hospital. It wasn't just the British who were wary of these women; the French were, too. Some of the women served as ambulance drivers and the French authorities were very reluctant to give them driving licences but eventually they had to concede that the 'girls in khaki could pilot their cars as well as any Frenchman'.

One visitor to the hospital wrote home describing the scene. Wards and beds were named after different Scottish people or places, he wrote:

'In the Ayr "Rabbie Burns" bed, was a clerical professor from Toulouse. I tried to impress on him the immense honour implied by giving him a bed with such a name. But he preferred to talk of G.K. Chesterton, whom he greatly admires... The nurses made me laugh when they told me of the French soldiers' fondness for pyjamas. Many of them had never seen such things until they came to the hospital, and when they were introduced to them, they found them so "chic" that some of them insisted on having two pairs; one for the ward and the other for promenading in the garden.'

As an administrator in charge of supplies for the hospital Katherine Harley regularly called on her friends and associates in Shropshire for help. In the *Chronicle* dated 14 May 1915 there is a letter from her asking for help:

'Clothing of all sorts, especially pyjamas and dressing gowns, will be required for our large family, but as the weather is warm, there will be no need for body belts, mittens or comforters. Cigarettes, biscuits and sweets are most welcome... I wish

I could adequately describe to your readers the patience and gratitude of these French soldiers and how much they are touched by the idea of English women leaving their homes to care for – not their own compatriots – but those of another nationality.' A month later the *Chronicle* notes the despatch to Mrs Harley's Hospital of '14 suits of pyjamas (material purchased by donations, and made up by members of the [Shrewsbury Branch of the Suffrage] society), 12 home-made cakes, nearly 5,000 cigarettes, also boxes of chocolates, fancy soaps, tins of biscuits etc.'

In October 1915 Katherine Harley travelled from France to the Balkans accompanied by forty nurses. In Salonika she and her contingent of nurses served in a 1,000 bed French hospital. She wasn't now just working with soldiers but also with women and children displaced by the war. She was then based in the town of Monastir which was under constant bombardment. Then on 7 March 1917, having spent the morning distributing food to the starving Serbians she was sitting by a window taking a brief tea break when shrapnel burst near the house and a fragment struck her. She was killed instantly.

Katherine Harley was a remarkable woman. Already in her sixties when she went out to serve with the Scottish Women's Hospitals, she was awarded the Croix de Guerre by the French government for her services to French soldiers. Following her death she was buried in the Military Cemetery in Thessalonika in Greece, the only woman to be buried there. A memorial was erected above her grave by the Serbs with an inscription (in two languages) which reads 'The generous English lady and great benefactress of the Serbian people, Madame Harley a great lady. On your tomb instead of flowers the gratitude of the Serbs shall blossom there for your wonderful acts. Your name shall be known from generation to generation.'

Back in Shrewsbury, on learning of her death, the *Chronicle* wrote:

'Shropshire women, and particularly those allied to the suffrage movement, are proud of Mrs Harley and of her heroic death while doing noble service in Monastir. In undertaking the work, Mrs Harley knew well the conditions were such that she

Plaque to Katherine Harley in the entrance of the former Royal Salop Infirmary.

was taking her life in her hands, and it is an open secret that some of her friends consider she should never have been sent to such a perilous post, and fruitlessly tried to dissuade her from undertaking it.'

Her name may not be so well known these days but she is still remembered in Shrewsbury with two memorials, one in St Mary's Church and one in the Parade, the former Royal Salop Infirmary. Perhaps her best memorial, however, was the annual award given to the most outstanding nurses when they completed their training in Shrewsbury.

Although the best known Shropshire woman to serve at the front during the Great War, Katherine Harley was by no means the only such lady. The distress of losing their husbands in the war caused a number of women to make the decision to serve in similar capacities. One such was was briefly mentioned in the *Chronicle* of 15 January 1916, when a sergeant serving in one of the Shrewsbury Pals battalions wrote home to say that he had met

'Mrs Pound, widow of the late Captain Pound, formerly of Shrewsbury School. I think it shows splendid spirit on the part of Mrs Pound, after having had her husband killed in action, to come out here voluntarily. I am sure, there must be quite a number of Shrewsbury and district ladies out here, and in other parts, engaged in hospital work, and I think it only fair that the fact should be brought to notice. I understand that they have to put in something like $10^{1}/_{2}$ hours a day out here, and they do it in the words of the old stock phrase as a "labour of love".'

Chapter Ten

The Wounded come to Shrewsbury

THE WAR HAD no sooner been declared than people began to raise funds to supply and support ambulances at the front. It wasn't long, either, before the wounded were being brought back to Blighty and not only the established hospitals but also temporary ones were prepared to receive them. The numbers are astounding, particularly when one considers that what was happening in Shrewsbury was being duplicated in towns all around the country.

As the Red Cross trains arrived at Shrewsbury Station they were met by teams of men and women who then escorted them on to hospitals throughout the county. Working out who went where must have been an horrendous task with the wounded men being divided into 'cot' cases and 'sitters' and passed on accordingly. This task was carried out by the Shrewsbury Volunteer Medical Corps working alongside such organizations as the St John's Ambulance Brigade and the Red Cross and they became extremely efficient. On one occasion, for example, an ambulance train arrived at the station with 142 patients at 5.30 pm and the last man left just an hour later (and there were 106 stretcher cases amongst this group, all of whom had to be carefully carried out and transferred into waiting vehicles).

In the single month of October 1917 it was estimated that the Volunteer Medical Corps, for example, had served 1,197 hours, of which 'hospital train duties' alone

The Royal Salop Infirmary. *(David Benson)*

amounted to 392 hours. (This did not include hours worked by officers, incidentally.) Red Cross trains were being processed regularly, sometimes with more than one ambulance train arriving within a single week. The men were then sent on, not just within Shrewsbury, but also to hospitals in Whitchurch, Much Wenlock, Oswestry, Market Drayton, Broseley – in fact all around Shropshire.

Obviously when the war broke out there were not enough hospitals to cope with such numbers and so additional hospitals were rapidly set up. In Shrewsbury many of these were in private houses around the town. The main hospital in Shrewsbury was the Royal Salop Infirmary which had been built in the 1830s as a subscription hospital for the townspeople. It was very modern for its time, it was one of the first hospitals in the country to have a hot water central heating system. But it had not been built for the influx of patients it now had to deal with. Indeed when war was declared the Infirmary immediately announced that it would reserve thirty beds for military cases. This soon was raised to fifty beds and then to sixty. This may, at first, seem a small number but, after all, this was the main hospital and continued to serve the community.

Another hospital that was soon inundated with some of the most badly wounded patients was the Baschurch Surgical Hospital. This had been founded primarily for children in 1900 in the village of Baschurch some eight miles north of Shrewsbury. It was originally intended as a convalescent home for the Salop Infirmary and was run by Agnes Hunt, whose family lived in the area. Agnes Hunt's own health, however, was poor so that she then consulted the orthopaedic surgeon, Robert Jones in Liverpool and soon afterwards in 1903 he agreed to come to Baschurch as the hospital's Honorary Surgeon. (With the outbreak of the war, Sir Robert Jones was appointed Inspector of Military Orthopaedics. His advocacy of the use of the Thomas splint for fractures caused by gunshots to the thigh reduced the morbidity rate of those with such wounds from eighty per cent to twenty per cent. He ended the war a major general and was knighted in 1917.)

Meanwhile, by 1907 an operating theatre had been built at Baschurch so that, when

Baschurch Surgical Hospital, now converted into apartments.
(The Robert Jones and Agnes Hunt Orthopaedic Hospital NHS Foundation Trust)

Patients at the Baschurch Surgical Hospital – notice the tent in the background; this was, in fact, one of the wards. *(The Robert Jones and Agnes Hunt Orthopaedic Hospital NHS Foundation Trust)*

war broke out in 1914, this was already a well-established surgical hospital. Then, in November 1914 the hospital was given two hours notice that the first thirty soldiers were on their way so that boys' wards had to be rapidly evacuated to make room for them.

Soldiers watching a sports day, Whit Monday 1917.
(The Robert Jones and Agnes Hunt Orthopaedic Hospital NHS Foundation Trust)

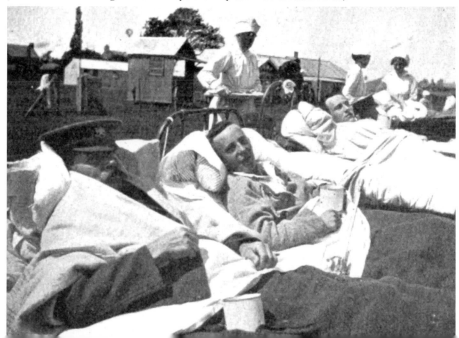

THIS HOUSE WAS THE CENTRE
OF THE FIRST OPEN-AIR HOSPIT
FOR CRIPPLES IN THE WORLD
FOUNDED IN 1900 BY
DAME AGNES HUNT, R.R.
THIS TABLET WAS ERECTED BY
BASCHURCH WOMENS' INSTITUTE T
CELEBRATE THE CORONATION O
QUEEN ELIZABETH II, JUNE 2ⁿᵈ 19

Plaque on the wall of the former Baschurch Surgical Hospital.

Inevitably there were problems with financing and at one point, realizing there was a need for the patients to have a new dining and recreation hall a local squad of men from the Shropshire Regiment, along with convalescent soldiers, came and did much of the work during their free time. Even the village blacksmith played his part – making splints for the patients.

Sir Robert Jones and Dame Agnes Hunt in the late 1920s. *(The Robert Jones and Agnes Hunt Orthopaedic Hospital NHS Foundation Trust)*

Dame Agnes Hunt (she was awarded the title in 1926) was an indefatigable woman. When there were lulls in the fighting and therefore fewer patients arriving, she would use the time to visit other local hospitals seeking out those patients she thought she could help. On one occasion she returned with a man who had been about to have both feet amputated. He was suffering from Trench Foot and his feet were black from frostbite. It took many weeks of suffering on the man's part but Dame Agnes Hunt not only saved his feet but got him walking again.

The hospital's fame spread throughout the country so that, according to one story in the *Chronicle*, a wounded soldier who had been recently discharged in Bournemouth and subsequently given employment in Shrewsbury said when told where he was being posted, 'Shrewsbury! Shrewsbury! Oh yes! That's the place near Baschurch, of course.' (It is worth bearing in mind that this reputation, gained in the Great War, still survives. The hospital moved in the 1920s to another site, near the village of Gobowen. It is now known as The Robert Jones and Agnes Hunt Orthopaedic Hospital and is considered one of the finest orthopaedic hospitals in the world.)

But these were not the only hospitals taking in war wounded in the Shrewsbury area. Many of the wounded were taken to private houses that had been converted for the purpose. These hospitals were generally known as Voluntary Aid Detachment (VAD) hospitals. This, as its name suggests, was a voluntary organization providing nursing care not just in hospitals within Britain but also in Europe and elsewhere. The organization had been founded in 1909. Nurses had to be at least twenty-three years of age and had to pass examinations in first aid. A VAD nurse was usually from a comfortable background (they had to be able to afford to buy their own uniforms for one thing, although as the war progressed and the need for nurses grew, these were later provided). The VAD hospitals were run with military precision (and discipline) with a hierarchy that included a Commandant and Quartermaster as well as the to-be-expected Matron, Sister and Nurse.

In Shrewsbury one such hospital was at Oakley Manor in Belle Vue. This hospital had space for forty-eight patients and the facilities to carry out operations. Similar hospitals were to be found in Quarry Place (seventy beds) and in Cyngfeld Auxiliary Military Hospital, Kingsland (fifty-eight beds).

But still these hospitals were not enough to cope with the flood of incoming patients. Consequently in 1916 the workhouse in the village of Berrington was requisitioned and fitted out as a new military hospital; the former inmates quarters were converted into wards and electric lighting was installed along with an X-Ray room and operation theatre. Once operational the Berrington War Hospital acted as a centre to which wounded soldiers were taken from the Red Cross trains and then subsequently transferred to other, smaller hospitals such as the one that opened at Attingham Park with its sixty beds. There were similar hospitals at Hodnet Hall which had an 'excellent billiard room' and at Oteley Park in Ellesmere where the patients were able to boat and fish, 'the rowing having been of real benefit in many cases'. Those soldiers who ended up at Stokesay Court near Ludlow were particularly well set up – nearly every man there had a room to himself. The hospital at Berrington, meantime, was the largest one in the

St John Auxiliary Military Hospital, now Prestfelde School. Notice the wounded soldiers standing in front of the entrance with nurses above them at the window. *(David Benson)*

Attingham Park; the Outer Library. *(The National Trust at Attingham Park)*

Shrewsbury district – on one occasion in 1917 it was able to receive 250 wounded soldiers 'in one batch' as the *Chronicle* described it.

But it wasn't just the physical wounds that were being treated at places such as Berrington. A great deal was done by local people who took the time to arrange entertainments for the men. Outings were arranged, with men being transported in charabancs or by pony and trap to local homes or for picnics by the river. Concerts were regularly held within the larger of the hospital wards.

And local people visited. One lady recalled how she asked one patient his age. 'Seventeen and a half,' the soldier replied, which, of course, was technically under-age for a soldier to be serving at the front. 'What age were you when you joined?' queried the lady. The soldier smiled and replied, 'You see, madam, I was older then!'

Attingham Park; beds along the open West Colonnade. *(The National Trust at Attingham Park)*

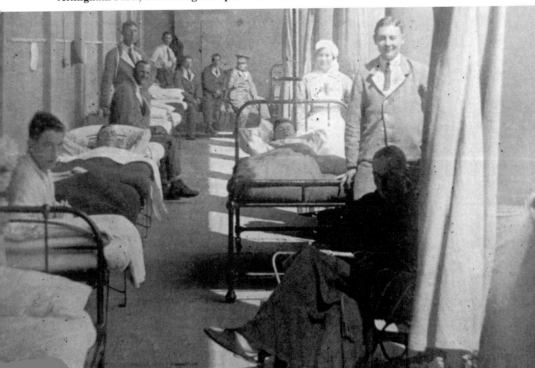

Chapter Eleven

The Introduction of Conscription

ALTHOUGH ENLISTMENT IN the British armed forces was historically entirely voluntary, white feathers and other methods of persuasion notwithstanding, by the latter part of 1915 the subject of conscription was coming more and more to the fore. The writer, Edgar Wallace, wrote regular articles on the subject of the war and these were syndicated in local papers around the United Kingdom. He was one of many influential people who advocated conscription although he was careful to stress its benefits for the men rather than the country when he wrote 'I must confess that I am a believer in conscription. There never was a man who had served in the army who did not believe… that soldiering is good for the manhood of the nation and for the discipline of the people.'

With the casualty lists always growing it was inevitable that in early 1916 conscription would be introduced. When the first call for men had gone out in August two years before, the requirements were quite clear – men should be aged between nineteen and thirty (although if ex-soldiers wished to rejoin they could do so up to the age of forty-two). They had to be at least 5ft 3in in height with a chest measurement not less than 34in. Single men were preferred although married men or widowers with children would also be accepted and, in their case, allowances would be paid to their families.

Bit by bit these stipulations came to be ignored so that eventually all men of military age who were not in reserved occupations had to make themselves available; by 1916 the Medical Boards were classifying men roughly into three groupings: those men fit for fighting, those who could undertake garrison duties somewhere abroad and those who would take on less arduous duties at home. The medicals soon became something of a battlefield in themselves, especially since local doctors usually carried them out. One man, on failing his medical complained to the doctor that 'you could have got me out of this, because you know I broke my ribs.'

"LOR! AND HERE TRIED FOR THIRTY YEARS, AND CAN'T GET ONE!"

Lor! And here I've tried for thirty years, and can't get one!

'Yes,' retorted his doctor, 'but that was four years ago, and I patched you up, and you've never been to me since or complained of your ribs until now.'

The call went out for an additional one million men. At first all men from the age of eighteen to forty had to be voluntarily attested – in other words they had to give an oath saying that they were ready to serve their country if they were called upon to do so. Their details were then given to their local recruitment boards so that they could be called up as required. Men who didn't register were liable for fines of up to £100 or six months imprisonment; and it wasn't just individuals either who were liable – businesses that didn't register all male employees between the ages of eighteen and forty-one could be fined up to £20.

If, once they were called up, any man wished to be exempted from service he then had to go before a tribunal stating why he felt he should be excused. Right from the start of conscription married men, in particular, were advised to apply for appeal forms ready for when they may be called up.

And so, in towns all around the country, tribunals were held to decide the fate of those men who wanted to appeal. It was something of a conveyor belt system with frequently anything up to sixty cases being heard in an afternoon. Very few men got a total exemption from service, most of them being only allowed to put off the date when they had to join up. Even those who were given exemption were liable to be re-examined should the government so decree. In most cases the best result a man could get would be to be allowed exemption for a limited time. Sometimes this amounted to only two or three weeks to, perhaps, enable a man to help get in the harvest, but an average in the Shrewsbury tribunals seems to have been somewhere in the range of three months. And then, when the time was up men either had to sign on or apply yet again for a further exemption. And these tribunals continued right up to the end of the war with, in October 1918, men still being given exemption that would take them into the next year. When the war was first declared many men had quickly got themselves married in the hope that this would enable them to stay at home. It didn't work once conscription began and, indeed, the tribunals were particularly strict with those men whose marriages had taken place after the war began.

We're proud of our boys here at SHREWSBURY

Our boys to history will go down,
The brightest jewels in Britain's crown.

1337

(David Benson)

Reports of the tribunals in the years that followed the introduction of conscription make harsh reading.

In Shrewsbury many of the people applying for exemption were farm workers such as the shepherd from Montford who was earning £1 a week and supported his seventy-year-old mother. There was a long discussion as to where the mother could go to live instead because, in the event that the shepherd was called up he would lose his tied cottage; the end result was that he was given a little time to get his mother settled first. (In fact there were a number of cases where concern was felt that the cottage that came with a job would be lost if the man was called up, and where then would his family live?). In a similar case another farmer, applying on behalf of one of his workers, told the court that he had already had to reduce his herd of Herefords by one fifth and if he lost this worker's skills, his business would be wrecked. Yet another farmer, claiming he needed a man to help with the milking, was told 'get children from the [village] school to help you'.

Many businesses struggled to survive. There are frequent notices in the paper announcing that this architect or that dentist, for example, is no longer available to serve his clients as he had been called up. There was the man running a furnishing business who was struggling to carry on after his father and three brothers had gone – the company had lost fourteen men who had enlisted. His was one case where an exemption was granted – perhaps because he had connections, as he also carried out haulage contracts, one of which was with the army camp at Prees Heath! Then there was the episode in one shop in Shrewsbury that was described in the *Chronicle* when a lady asked for a repair man to be sent 'at once' to her house. 'I'm sorry,' the manager replied, 'but it cannot be done. The fact is our "at once" man is in the Trenches!'

People in businesses such as this were often advised to take on women to replace the men who had gone but this was not always successful. One baker, for example said that he supplied bread to the PoW camp in Shrewsbury and could not employ women to deliver it because they would not be allowed to pass the gates. Similarly, when a provision dealer was told he should employ women to replace the men he wanted to keep, he said they would not be strong enough. One of the men on the tribunal then commented that, as he came along the High Street that day he had seen two women lifting a heavy sofa off a cart in the street. The dealer, however, insisted that that was 'nothing compared to lifting whole cheeses and sides of bacon'. He lost his appeal.

Pacifists and Conscientious Objectors

Such was the odium felt towards such men, it took courage of a different kind from that needed on the front to be a Conscientious Objector in the Great War. Typical of the reaction to such people was a letter written in the satirical magazine *The Wipers Times* that was produced by men who were actually fighting in France and Belgium. 'Sir,' it stated, 'I read in the papers that a star is being granted for the men who fought in 1914. As one of the earliest conscientious objectors (I discovered my conscience on August 5th 1914) I must ask you to obtain for us some special recognition. Surely you cannot but admire the struggle we have put up against the overstrong odds of a sensitive conscience, and that we have been defeated is no fault of ours.'

Not all conscientious objectors found their conscience only after the war broke out, by any means. But this did not help them much once they were called up and went before the tribunals. One of the few cases in Shrewsbury where an exemption was given concerned a man who had been a member of the Plymouth Brethren since 1906 – but he was only given exemption on the understanding that he found work in a certified (reserved) occupation. And it must be said, of course, that many conscientious objectors did serve at the front, often as stretcher bearers, and many died whilst carrying out their duties.

Chapter Twelve

Soldiers in the sky - the formation of the Flying Corps

THE FIRST WORLD War was the first war in which air combat played an important role. It was not entirely new, however. Incredible though it is to believe nowadays, aerial reconnaissance began in the French Revolutionary Wars of the 1790s with the use of observation balloons – ballooning was a French idea after all. Again balloons were used in the American Civil War and then their importance grew immensely when Paris was besieged during the Franco-Prussian War when they were used by the Parisians to send messages from the beleaguered city. Once again, in the First World War they were used for observation purposes; the phrase 'the balloon's going up' dates from the fact that these balloons allowed the enemy to pinpoint targets, often ones that could not be seen by ground-based artillery, and so direct their bombardment.

But the First World War saw a new use for aerial warfare. Planes could be used to drop bombs. The first bomb ever to fall in Britain was dropped – literally, the pilot had to pick it up and drop it over the side of his plane – in Dover on Christmas Eve in 1914. There were no casualties although the shock caused a gardener to fall out of the tree he was pruning. Some three weeks later two Zeppelins targeted Great Yarmouth and King's Lynn and four people were killed. Such attacks had already been envisaged and discussed at conventions at The Hague in 1899 and again in 1907. A prohibition of such attacks had been suggested but since Germany had not signed any such agreement

Inside a hangar on the Shawbury air base. *(RAF Shawbury)*

Sopwith Camel on the grass runway. *(RAF Shawbury)*

and the wording of the suggested agreement was somewhat ambiguous it was generally considered that such attacks would be legitimate. When bombs had been dropped on Paris in September 1914 the then pro-German *New York Herald* described the bombing as a 'triumph for German culture' although they might have changed their tune somewhat had the American ambassador been killed – apparently he just missed the attack by minutes.

Paris was just behind the western front. England, however, had a sea between it and

the fighting so that when English coastal towns were attacked the panic that this caused amongst the population at home can only be imagined. Laws were introduced immediately to combat the risk of air raids and these were nationwide; even a town like Shrewsbury was affected. Within days of the first Zeppelin attack Shrewsbury was in 'a state of semi-darkness and the market clock and other prominent landmarks were devoid of illumination'. Some people were even saying that they saw an airship pass over the town one night.

It seems astounding that people in Shrewsbury should have been affected by this panic and its reaction but, in fact, there was good reason for it. It was not just the coast that bore the brunt of the attacks, towns in the Midlands such as Burton-on-Trent and Walsall were attacked and, on occasion, Zeppelins even reached as far as Manchester and Liverpool. In one attack in the Midlands it was reported that eleven people were killed and entire streets devastated. And so the Local Volunteer Corps was trained in how to deal with the dropping of incendiary devices.

Everyone started buying material to darken their windows and the blackout regulations were strictly enforced so that there were, in the *Chronicle* for the next two years, frequent court cases concerning people showing a light. The cases varied and the fines given out ranged from five shillings to ten. Flora Winslow, for example, was fined ten shillings when she failed to shade the light in her bedroom at the sanatorium at Shrewsbury School one night – apparently the light was so bright it 'shone like a big star'. Not everyone was fined. A dental surgeon who, when his case came to court, pleaded that he had been urgently called away from the premises where the light was on because his wife was dangerously ill, asked the Bench to withdraw the case. It did. Such

Kingsland Bridge from above.

pleas didn't always work and, as time passed, more and more of the defendants in these cases were charged ten shillings although there was the occasional caution given instead.

Meanwhile the British were developing their own air army. In June 1917 a flying training station was established for the new Royal Flying Corps just a few miles out of Shrewsbury beside the village of Shawbury.

Those young pilots learning to fly at Shawbury were soon demonstrating their skills in the air above Shrewsbury. In July 1917 there were a couple of such exhibitions above the town, one of which was subsequently described in the *Chronicle*:

'Salopians were privileged to witness a sensational display of flying on Monday evening by an intrepid airman, who manoeuvred a powerful biplane in so daring a manner that his thrilling feats must have been seen to be believed possible. The exhibition lasted upwards of half an hour, and the weather conditions were ideal. The airman looped the loop times out of number, fled upside down, and indulged in a variety of apparently reckless antics at high and low altitudes which practically unnerved many eye-witnesses. Once the biplane seemed to be tumbling to earth in corkscrew fashion, and a wounded soldier on Pride Hill cried, "He's done it this time! Five shillings to a pinch of snuff, he's down." The next instant, however, the airman was gracefully soaring up again, with a view to providing more, and still more thrills. The performance won the admiration of the boys at Shrewsbury School, the crowd of people at the Quarry concerts, and hundreds of people gathered at every vantage point in the borough. It was an intense relief to many when the marvellous exploits terminated, and the airman flew for home.'

A week later a boat race was being held at Shrewsbury School and rumours started to circulate through the town that there was going to be another flying display. Crowds began to gather in the Quarry Gardens. The boat race was already underway when two bi-planes arrived but much to the disappointment of the crowd the pilots merely landed in the school grounds. The crowd waited and their patience was finally rewarded when the show began, the culmination of the display being when one pilot flew under the Kingsland Bridge eight times in all.

Then there was the pilot who decided to pop up to Wem from his base in the Berkshire to visit a girlfriend. She was obviously expecting him because, as his plane appeared, she waved to let him know where he was. But then he needed to find somewhere to land and ended up making a rather messy landing in a wheat field nearby. The machine was slightly damaged but fortunately some mechanics from nearby Shawbury were able to repair it so that his return flight wasn't too much postponed.

But it wasn't long before there were fatalities, too. Training was then so lacksadaisical that more pilots died whilst being trained than when fighting. Another major problem was that the early pilots weren't usually equipped with parachutes – at least, not the British pilots. German pilots, on the other hand, did have them so that it's interesting to note that when a certain Herman Goering crash landed his plane over the western front he was able to escape in good time.

Despite this, it's no wonder that the Royal Air Force (which was established on 1 April 1918 when the Royal Flying Corps was transformed into a service of its own) became a boy's dream of an elite career within the military. As one pilot later said, 'I'd been in the infantry and we were always lousy, filthy, dirty and very often hungry, whereas in the Flying Corps it's a gentleman's life'.

There is one particularly fascinating letter in the *Chronicle* advocating the RAF as a career. It is printed in the paper as a 'letter' but it would be much more accurate to say that this is a career advertisement. The writer is an air mechanic advising a friend on the possibilities of such a career for his son who is just about to reach military age.

What I find particularly fascinating about this 'letter' is not so much the blatant RAF propaganda as the way in which it describes the career possibilities once the war has ended for people with such training, and in this it seems to be extremely accurate and far-sighted:

'Harry [the son of the man to whom the mechanic is writing] will learn more in six months in the Air Force than in years and years of plumbing. It is very interesting work. You do not seem able to help getting keen on it. Some jobs are dull because you never see why you do them. You do not work blindly at an aerodrome, and very soon after you have done it you see your work in mid air, and I assure you, you watch its doings there with interest.

'Why I would put my son to the Air Force is because flying is the one thing that is certain to be bigger after the war than it is today. The man who knows the ins and outs of aeroplanes is the man who is going to find the best kind of jobs waiting for him after the war. War flying is big, and I should not wonder if flying does not

Kingland Bridge - there's not much space for any plane to fly below.

Sopwith Camel in the hangar for maintenance. *(RAF Shawbury)*

end the war; but peace flying will be a lot bigger than war flying.

'War flying means flying in Europe, and peace flying means flying from end to end of the British Empire.'

Which, of course, turned out to be very true. Though it was not immediately apparent in Shawbury's case. The airfield there was closed down in 1920 and the land reverted to agricultural use once again. However, the site was reactivated as an airfield in 1938 and has continued as such ever since.

Chapter Thirteen

Wilfred Owen

THERE WERE MANY Shrewsbury men from all walks of life who deserve special mention. However one man stands out, not because of anything he did at the time but, rather, because of the influence he would have over the generations that followed. That man was, of course, the poet, Wilfred Owen. Not that he was deemed to be anything special at the time since only his close family and friends then knew anything of his poetry. It was not until 1920, after the war ended, that his work was first published along with an introduction by the much-better-known-at-the-time Siegfried Sassoon whom Owen had met during the war.

Wilfred Owen was born in Oswestry in 1893, of mixed English-Welsh ancestry. Perhaps that explains the mastery of his work – the combination of the rich English language with the Celtic sense of music in the way words are used. His father, Thomas Owen, worked for the London and North Western and Great Western Railways, serving on stations used by the companies and in 1900 the family moved to Birkenhead when Thomas Owen was appointed as Station Master at Woodside station. Then in 1907 Thomas was transferred to Shrewsbury and the family then went to live in Monkmoor Road.

The house on Monkmoor Road where the Owen family lived. *(Shropshire Archives)*

Wilfred was still only about ten or eleven when he discovered his love of poetry so that he was already dabbling with writing as he attended the Shrewsbury Technical School. On finishing his formal education he served as a pupil-teacher in a school in Wyle Cop, working meantime for a matriculation exam in order to attend the University of London. He passed the exam but failed to attain the first-class pass he needed in order to get the scholarship so that he could afford to go. Instead he got a post as a tutor in the village of Dunsden near Reading in return for free lodging and, while living there, he attended classes at the University College in Reading.

As a young boy his

Plaque on the Monkmoor Road House.

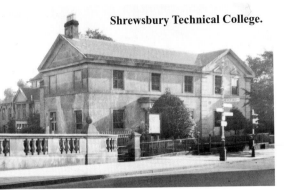

Shrewsbury Technical College.

father had taken him to France, a country he soon fell in love with, and in 1913, following a serious illness, he decided to find work in France and so avoid the English winter. Little did he realize that one day he would write 'I shall never again beg father to take me to France'. Thus, when the war broke out in August the following year he was working as a tutor teaching English and French at the Berlitz School of Languages in Bordeaux. He didn't return to England immediately; perhaps, like so many, he assumed it would be 'all over by Christmas' and there would have been little point. But the following year it was evident that the war would continue for some time and, having briefly considered joining the French army, he returned to England to enlist.

By the end of 1915 Owen was serving with the Artists' Rifles Officers' Training Corps. (Incidentally, the Artists' Rifles came to be nicknamed the Suicide Club because such a large proportion of the men who joined subsequently became commissioned officers and so were in the front line in battle.) In the *Chronicle* in June 1916 it was stated that 'Mr Wilfred Owen, eldest son of Mr T. Owen, Assistant to the Joint Railway Superintendent, Shrews, has been given a Commission in the 3/5 Manchester Regiment, at present in camp at Milford Surrey. At the outbreak of the war Lieut Owen was in Bordeaux, engaged as a tutor, and after fulfilling his engagement returned to England and joined the Artists' Rifles OTC last September, passing successfully from the School three weeks ago.'

Gazetted to the 2nd Battalion of the Manchester Regiment he arrived in France full of excitement at the prospect of the experiences to come. Writing home to his mother soon afterwards he said 'This morning I was hit! We were bombing, and a fragment from somewhere hit my thumb knuckle. I coaxed out one drop of blood. Alas! No more!! There is a fine heroic feeling about being in France, and I am in perfect spirits.'

Unfortunately, there was little that was fine or heroic about trench warfare. In the months that followed, besides living for days on end in trenches full of water, Owen was to suffer concussion in a shell hole, be blown into the air by a mortar and then, at one point, he lay 'in a railway cutting, in a hole just big enough to lie in, and covered with corrugated iron. My brother officer… lay in a similar hole. But he was covered with earth, and no relief will ever relieve him.' Eventually he was diagnosed as suffering from shellshock and returned to Britain and it was then that he met Siegfried Sassoon, also recuperating.

He returned to the front line in August 1918 and it was on 4 November that he was shot and killed. The following day he would have received news of his promotion to the rank of Lieutenant. His family instead received the dreaded telegram on Armistice Day itself.

Memorial by Shrewsbury Abbey. It bears the words 'I am the enemy you killed, my friend' from Owen's poem *Strange Meeting*.

Chapter Fourteen

Fighting Germans, Austrians and Drink

MANY PEOPLE ARE aware that the licensing hours in our pubs today derive largely from David Lloyd George who, as Chancellor in March 1915, spoke the words, 'We are fighting Germany, Austria and drink; and as far as I can see, the greatest of these deadly foes is drink.'

In fact drunkenness had been a perennial problem for years. Any local newspaper in the years leading up to the war is full of references to court cases dealing with drunks and Shrewsbury's local paper is no different. Some hundred years earlier the Temperance Movement had started to grow in popularity and in Shrewsbury one leading exponent had been the wife of the vicar of St Alkmund's, Julia Wightman. Mrs Wightman had often watched as the wives of workmen would gather on a Friday afternoon outside the buildings in which their husbands received their pay, ready to waylay the men as they

Golden Cross Passage Shrewsbury.

The Golden Cross pub.

emerged in order to get what money they could from them before the men headed for the nearest pub where they would otherwise spend their entire week's earnings in one long drinking bout.

It was in the 1860s that Mrs Wightman achieved her ambition and finally opened a non-alcoholic pub or, to be more precise, a Working Men's Hall as it was called at the time. Ironically, the previous building on the site had been a pub that had a notorious reputation for the heavy drinking of its customers. Coming on the market Mrs Wightman had, with her own money, bought it for the then enormous sum of £700 and had her own hall built instead. Once the Hall opened it was not simply a venue for non-alcoholic beverages but also meals could be obtained, there was a reading room with newspapers, lectures were held… in fact everything was done that could be done to encourage customers and it proved to be very successful.

Not that it stopped all the drinking problems of the town.

With the outbreak of war licensing hours were limited. Before then pubs would often open first thing in the morning (to supply drink to those on their way to work) and stay open until midnight. The new laws, which were not particularly successful, stated that they could only open for a maximum of six hours per day with a break at some point in the afternoon.

Although a national law, it was up to local authorities to put it into practice and this cannot have been easy in those early months of the war when large groups of soldiers were billeted upon towns around the country where, in what spare time they had, there was nothing for them to do but go to the pubs. One letter to the *Chronicle* in November 1914 comments, however, that: 'The action of the Shrewsbury Licensing Bench in curtailing the hours of opening of licensed houses and clubs is a curious commentary on the compliment paid to the town by the Borough Recorder, at the Quarter Sessions, on Friday, who pointed out that, in spite of the fact that so many soldiers had been quartered in the town during the last three months, there had been a very sensible decrease in the number of offences, and that drunkenness, which might have been expected to show a considerable increase, was practically stationary.

'The public generally are prepared to exercise some self-denial at this crisis, but they need to be on their guard lest extremists take advantage of the troublous times to force legislation which would not be tolerated in ordinary circumstances. (signed) Tolerance.'

Tolerance could obviously see what lay ahead. Drinking restrictions continued to be imposed. A year later the military authorities ordered that all public houses within the county should close at 9.00pm; an hour earlier than previously. This was to cause one woman a problem the following spring when she forgot that the clocks had just been changed. The story appears in the *Chronicle* under the heading *Shrewsbury Woman's*

String of Horses pub, now in the Avoncroft Museum of Historic Buildings.

Terrible Plight! Apparently she had been attending a concert in the Quarry and had been so entranced by the music that it was only when she heard the clock of Shrewsbury School chiming the hour that she realized it was nine o'clock and she had therefore missed her chance to get her beer before supper. 'Mother,' her son retorted when he heard her complaint, 'you will be beerless tonight!'

Limited drinking hours were not enough for some of the local temperance leaders who, at a meeting in July 1916, adopted a resolution in which they urged the Government to 'prohibit the manufacture, import, export and sale of intoxicating liquors during the war and for six months afterwards'. A correspondent, calling himself 'Moderation', replied in a letter to the *Chronicle* that he had only the other day asked an engineer in Shropshire, employing nearly a 1,000 men 'Have you any trouble from drinking?' The man replied that he had 'only one fellow who takes too much and he is one of my best men.'

The Government wasn't content with simply restricting the drinking hours, however, and, in April 1917, they decided to reduce the output of beer by 70 per cent in the financial year just begun. Wines and spirits were to be restricted, too. The next move was to lessen the alcoholic content of what beers were still being produced.

People still managed to get more than enough to drink though and court cases dealing with drunks were still regularly mentioned in the paper. Soldiers home on leave often managed to get their cases dismissed, sometimes with a caution. Thomas Green was one such example – he was a private in the KSLI and was found by a constable lying helpless in Wyle Cop with a half-full bottle of whisky in his possession. His excuse was that he had come to Shrewsbury on furlough and, having been teetotal all the time he was away had taken 'a drop of whisky'.

Similarly Edward Griffiths who was charged with being drunk in the High Street told the court that, having served six months in France, he came to Shrewsbury to be medically examined, when he met some friends and had only 'two glasses of beer, and it got to him', was discharged with a caution.

Women, however, could not use the same excuse although Annie Barker, who lived in Castle Fields, tried a similar defence. The case was described in the paper as follows: 'PC Edwards said he found Barker lying down very drunk. He picked her up, and she became so violent that witness had to obtain assistance and convey the defendant in a handcart to the police station. Barker's behaviour all the way to the police station was disgraceful. PC Peacock and Inspector Frank Davies gave corroborative evidence. Defendant

said she was not drunk. She had been out working all day, and had only had one drink. She had five sons and four sons-in-law fighting, but she had the biggest brute of a husband in the world. Defendant called her daughter, Emily Twyford, but although this witness said her mother was not as drunk as the police made out, she had to admit that the defendant was not sober. Defendant was fined 6s.'

One law passed by the Government to control drinking, and it must have been almost impossible to control, was the Treating Order. It came into force in many parts of Britain in September 1916 and stated that it was illegal for one person to buy another a drink; the only exception was when the drink was part of a meal that was being purchased. In Southampton there was even a court case when a man was tried for the crime of buying his wife a drink. (Incidentally both he and his wife were found guilty and fined.)

In Shrewsbury Sarah Lewis, landlady of the Britannia Hotel (now the Shrewsbury Hotel), found herself in court for just this crime when she served a drink to George Lloyd, a farmer from Aston-on-Clun, that had been paid for by another farmer, Knowlson Hignett, of Myddle. It's an interesting case. The solicitor representing Mrs Lewis said that he would like to offer an apology on her behalf and went on to explain that 'she had been serving beer upstairs in the dining room, where they were allowed to treat friends when supplied with meals. It was more absent-mindedness than anything else that caused her to allow Hignett to treat his friend.'

Her solicitor's pleas seem to have worked because, although the judge expressed his view that this was a very serious offence, Mrs Lewis was fined £2. That wasn't all, however. The two men were also charged, one with the crime of buying another man a drink and the other with drinking a drink he had not bought himself. Both defendants pleaded guilty but 'explained that as they lived in the countryside where the no-treating order was not in force, they were not aware that they were doing wrong.' Their cases were dismissed but they still had to pay costs.

Believe it not, Mrs Lewis was back in court some four months later facing the same charge although this time it was not she who had served the men but her barmaid whose excuse was that she didn't know just which man it was who had put the money on the bar. The fines were rather higher this time – the barmaid paid costs, Mrs Lewis was fined £2 for each of the charges brought against her (there were several), two of the men involved were fined 10 shillings, one had to pay costs and those men who were not local had their cases dismissed.

Chapter Fifteen

SOS – Save or Starve

WAR WAS DECLARED on 4 August 1914. In the *Chronicle* dated 7 August there are already reports of panic buying in the shops to such an extent that 'several principal stores had to close their doors until the orders they had in hand could be executed'. But the panic didn't last for long. Everyone knew there was really no need for panic because the war would be over by Christmas. (Everyone, that is, except Lord Kitchener who anticipated that it would last for three years or so.)

The United Kingdom, with the support of the British Empire all around the world, didn't at first need to worry about the food supply. After the Battle of Jutland in May 1916, however this became a severe problem for Germany when all their ports were blockaded by the Royal Navy. The Germans, however, retaliated with their U-boats and in the months that followed the British finally began to feel the effects of this aspect of warfare. By 1917 the situation was becoming dire. Indeed, in the month of April 1917 German U-boats sank twenty-five per cent of all the ships that left British ports.

At first the Government appealed to the better nature of the public, simply asking that they should lessen the amount of food they ate. For example in December 1916 the Board of Trade ordered that there should be limits to the meals served in all public eating places – no longer could people have three-course meals. This order was rapidly followed by another prohibiting the eating of meal or poultry or game on certain days of the week. There were appeals to the public to 'refrain from using essential foods' at events such as 'whist drives, Parochial or Church teas, dances, or any other form of entertainment, whether organized in the name of charity or not'.

But it was quickly realized that simply appealing to the public's better nature would not work. Prices were rising steadily which meant that the poorer people soon struggled to get even the basics. Some fairer system of food distribution had to be introduced. And so, in February 1917, rationing limiting the amount of bread, meat and sugar people could buy was introduced, although at this stage it was still voluntary. An

Lord Kitchener.

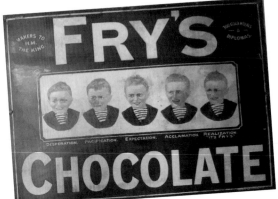

announcement in the *Chronicle* warned, however, that Lord Devonport, the Food Controller, asked 'the nation on its honour to observe the conditions' and stated that meanwhile 'the machinery to bring such a system [of rationing] into operation is being organized, so that it may be ready if and when required. Lord Devonport makes a special appeal to the women to exercise economy.' So everyone had been warned.

In December 1917 a *Save or Starve* week was announced during which everyone in the country was expected to make some sacrifice in the amount of food they consumed. But this didn't work either so that regulations were steadily tightened. Flour mills were taken under government control; dog biscuits were only to be made from low-grade millers' offal which wasn't suitable for humans. One regulation stated that potatoes could only be eaten on Friday. Indeed on one occasion there was such a rush for new potatoes in Shrewsbury market that fighting broke out and policemen had to be called to form up the crowd in a reasonable queue. People were encouraged to seek alternatives for their tables and you regularly see announcements for demonstrations, for example, on the bottling of fruit and vegetables.

The prospect of rationing came ever closer. Already in September 1917 people had been encouraged to register with their local retailers so that when rationing was introduced they would be ready for it. In this instance it was a sugar registration card people had to apply for – these would arrive in the post or forms could be obtained from any post office. The form, once completed then had to be deposited with the grocer of your choice who would then receive the amount of sugar required for the number of people registered with him.

Not everyone was happy with these arrangements and some time later there appeared in the *Chronicle* the, to my mind, most wonderful letter, which I can only reprint in full:

'Sir, As I am, unfortunately, one of the inquisitive sex, I should like to know why I am compelled to furnish my local grocer with the year of my birth in order to be favoured with a paltry half-pound of sugar per week. I am already of a very sweet disposition, and do not feel inclined to give away one of my cherished secrets in order to ensure any further fragrance in that respect. If I had any desire to publish the figure I daresay I could confide in my charwoman with a certainty of being not later than a week behind the grocer's confidential communication to others.

'Had I been ushered into the world with masculine virtues and patriotic

leanings, I could probably have hid in a funk-hole until ferreted out, and then have gone whining to the local Tribunal, which ought not to exist, for exemption; and all this without my name even being mentioned in your widely circulated paper. Probably, too, I could have shared in the mis-management of the nation's domestic affairs, instead of having to sign myself, 'A Disgusted Female'.

It has to be pointed out that the accompanying comment from the Editor states that

'It does not seem possible to the lay mind that the age of every consumer should be necessary before ½lb of sugar is allowed. If this information is required for any ulterior object, why cannot those who are responsible for what looks like an irrelevant and impertinent question be honest enough to say so?'

He then goes on to add that

'our correspondent is, however, in error in supposing that the information necessarily comes before the grocer. If the tickets are sent in a sealed packet to the grocer they are handed to the official of the Food Control Committee unopened; and the officials are pledged to secrecy.'

But I'm not too sure that that would have satisfied this lady.

By early 1918, however, the situation really was serious. And it wasn't just sugar that was rationed. Not surprisingly, those who could afford it began hoarding food and this, as much as anything else, necessitated the introduction of rationing of numerous other products.

Already in January the Shrewsbury Food Committee had announced that the Ministry of Food had cut the amount of meat available for sale by half so that all butchers had to themselves ration what they sold. The idea was that the butchers, knowing what their customers usually bought, would limit them to half their normal order. Furthermore, customers who wanted, say, a leg of mutton, might well have to make do with ribs of beef or whatever … Customers, too, were warned that they would not be able to evade these restrictions by going around other butchers' shops since the butchers were told they could only serve their regulars.

What with the problems at the butchers' shops, people looked to other sources of meat – rabbits for example. Shrewsbury's mayor, Councillor Morris, sent a letter to the *Chronicle* asking all farmers in the area to please help the situation by supplying rabbits for the market. This prompted a comment in a later paper remarking on the abundance of rabbits on Haughmond Hill leading the writer to wonder at the shortage in the town's market. Pork was an alternative meat and so rules were relaxed allowing people to rear their own pigs and that, provided permission was obtained from the local authority, no place could be considered unsuitable for keeping pigs, provided they did not cause nuisance to neighbours. The allotment holders in Cherry Orchard can't have been the only group to establish a Pig Club; in this case they commandeered a local old age pensioner to look after their eleven pigs.

It wasn't long before other food products were added to the list of those that were rationed. Dairy products were a problem. The price of milk had been rising steadily (already there had been cases of farmers selling adulterated milk – one case concerned a farmer who had sold milk which was twenty per cent added water) and a scheme was introduced giving priority for infants and invalids to receive milk before other customers were supplied. Even farmers who produced their own butter and sold it to neighbours were regulated. Bread obviously was a problem, since cereals had to be imported, but even vegetables were limited. A delightfully named *British Onions Order* stipulated that no person, except a dealer, 'may buy more than 7lbs in one week and no dealer may sell more than 7lbs a week to any household, institution or catering business'.

In fact, there were so many restrictions that many people must have been utterly confused. They caused one elderly lady to visit the Ministry of Food office in Shrewsbury to discuss a problem that concerned her. 'When I die,' she told an official, 'I should like my funeral to be properly carried out.' She then went on to say that she had carefully prepared for the event by storing her coffin, her shroud, two bottles of whisky and three tins of salmon. Was this permissible? She was most relieved when told that this would be fine 'so long as she did not add to her stock'.

Winning the War in the Kitchen

There was for a time a series of *Splendid Saving Hints for Housewives* that was syndicated in newspapers nationwide. Housewives were asked to send in their ideas and the writers of those that were published received the grand sum of half a crown (12^1/$_2$p). These hints can only amuse us today but, at the same time, they give a very clear picture of the difficulties encountered by everyone at the time.

Mrs Davidson won her 2/6 when she suggested: 'When cutting the bread or teacake for the family breakfast, or tea, save the crumbs in a small basin. When the basin is full crush them then put in a jar for puddings. A good amount soon gathers, and these dried crumbs may be used for all puddings for which bread would ordinarily be required'.

Another winning suggestion was to use parsnips when making bread in order to eke out the flour ration. People were reminded, when peas were plentiful in the summer, not to waste them. At Christmas time there was another reminder that the mince pies that everybody always ate would be unobtainable since the flour, the sugar, and the dried fruits required for them all had to be imported.

An idea to stretch the butter allowance suggested that:

'for every half-pound of butter [you will need] half a pint of new milk and a small spoonful of salt. Heat the milk to blood heat, add the salt, and pour it into a basin; break the butter up with a fork, and heat in the warm milk into the consistency of Devonshire cream. Set aside to cool. The butter will not keep for more than a week… but every half pound of butter will weigh nearly a pound.'

But my favourite suggestion of all came from an 'elderly officer' who wrote:

'Many old gentlemen like myself have been accustomed to drinking a glass or two of whisky every night before going to bed. I now drink green ginger wine, with hot or cold water instead, and find it an excellent substitute, and a great saving in money. I go to my work all the better in the morning for the change'.

Chapter Sixteen

Prisoners of War

THE FIRST PRISONERS of war were not prisoners as a result of any fighting. As happened immediately war was declared in 1939, so too, in 1914 were all enemy aliens in Britain immediately taken into custody. An Aliens Registration Act was promptly passed in Parliament and this gave the government power to control, not just Germans but people of all nationalities. Regarding the Germans, however, many were instructed to leave and over 20,000 of them did just that. Those who stayed were told to register with their local authorities and risked a fine of £100 (an enormous sum at the time) or imprisonment for six months.

Many of those who remained in the UK were then placed in internment camps where they were checked out before, in most cases, being allowed back into the community. It should be noted that, at the time of the outbreak of war, German people made up the third largest immigrant group in Britain (after Irish and Jewish communities). In fact it was later to become a running joke amongst soldiers in the trenches that if one shouted out 'Waiter!' a dozen heads would pop up in the German trenches to answer 'Yes, sir!'

With the outbreak of war suspicion of all Germans (and, it must be said, people who might be German) intensified. This was nothing new. In fact, such feelings had been growing over the previous forty to fifty years due largely, to the development of a single German state under Chancellor Bismarck with an industrial might that rivalled Britain's own. Furthermore, once Kaiser Wilhelm came to the throne Germany began to have imperialistic ambitions that rivalled those of Britain's and to further those imperialistic ambitions the Kaiser had gone to extreme lengths to develop a navy that also was in direct competition to Britain's Royal Navy. With the outbreak of war between the nations all these rivalries and the nervousness of the British regarding the protection of their interests came to a head.

Reading what is only a local paper like the *Chronicle* one gets an inkling of this nervousness over German ambitions even in the months before war broke out. There are a number of references to German industrial developments although one reference in April 1914 takes a different viewpoint. It is titled *Germany's Eyes on Ulster* and goes on to say:

'at first sight the allegation may cause us some uneasiness, if not alarm; but it need not. The somewhat disturbing phrase does not mean that the Germans are casting hungry eyes on the Emerald Isle, but in the light of the events of the past few months in and around Belfast are beginning to regard England's troubles as a warning against democracy and against Parliamentary domination. We cannot object to that. If Germany or any other country is learning a lesson from the Irish question, we cannot find fault.'

The superior tone of this article is far removed from other reactions that seem to indicate a much deeper nervousness. One result of this when war eventually broke out was the reaction to anything German in the minds of people all over the country – German composers were suddenly no longer part of the repertoire of any orchestra; our Royal family changed their name to Windsor; German measles was renamed Belgian flush; perhaps one of the most long-lasting effects was the change of the name of German Shepherd dogs to Alsations so that to this day people are often confused and think they are two separate breeds.

With such nervousness there can be no surprise at the immediate establishment of internment camps for those Germans who decided to stay in the country. There was one such camp in Shrewsbury with men from all walks of life. Many of the men who were interned had married English girls and settled here with their families. This was the case with Ernst Koanig who found himself in court in Liverpool after he escaped from the Shrewsbury camp. Koanig's defence was that he could not bear being away from his wife and children:

'I had heard nothing of them for three days,' he said when questioned in court 'and it made me so uneasy I could not sleep at nights; so I walked through the gates and came to Liverpool to see them. I afterwards reported myself to the police here. I did not think of the seriousness of the thing when I left Shrewsbury. Before I went to the camp I had a permit to reside in Liverpool but things went badly. I got out of employment, and had to sell up my home. I reported myself to the police in order that I might be sent to the camp. My wife was to get assistance from the American Consul. For three days I did not hear from her, and I got uneasy.'

What made matters worse in Koanig's case was the fact that, by returning to Liverpool, he had gone to an area that was now prohibited to aliens but the judge, when sentencing him, acknowledged that following his return to Liverpool he had never endeavoured to conceal himself and mitigating circumstances in the case enabled Koanig to escape a long prison sentence.

It was not long, however, before true prisoners of war were placed in custody in the camp in Shrewsbury. Koanig was not the only prisoner to escape from the camp. On one occasion two prisoners escaped 'in broad daylight'; many people in the town saw them but at first the military authorities didn't broadcast news of the escape and so no-one realized that they were escapees. After a day on the run the authorities decided to issue a description of the two men so that they were captured that same evening.

The next two prisoners to escape made it all the way to Hull before they were recaptured. One of them was a ship's captain who had lived in Hull before the war. He and the sailor with him had been captured after the Battle of Jutland. The captain, whose wife had died some time before, had travelled to Germany a couple of weeks before the outbreak of the war. On his escape he had thought that former friends in Hull would help to smuggle him aboard a steamer to reach the Continent. His hopes were misplaced and instead he was betrayed to the police and recaptured.

Some prisoners do seem to have

THE END OF A PERFECT · DAY.

(Shropshire Regimental Museum)

Prisoners in the PoW camp near the Abbey, the tower of which can be seen in the background. *(Shropshire Archives)*

managed a successful escape. It happened in February 1918 when the River Rea was in flood so that three men one night managed to swim across. Descriptions of the men were immediately issued including the fact that only one of then could speak any English. There is no reference in the paper to the men being recaptured so perhaps they managed to get completely away. There was one amusing incident associated with that escape, however, that was reported in the *Chronicle*. It seems that a tramp was sleeping rough when he was hailed by one of the search parties. Fearing that he would be taken into custody he bolted and although the search party gave chase was never caught.

Two more prisoners escaped in June 1918. They were airmen, one of whom had been awarded the Iron Cross, and their escape was rather cleverly thought out. Being the middle of the summer the fireplace in their prison quarters (converted carriage works in the Abbey PoW Camp) was not being used and so they climbed up inside the chimney stack and got onto the roof and from there somehow managed to get out of the camp by cutting some wire netting at the top. They were well prepared for their escape, both being dressed in civilian clothing and carrying portmanteaux containing food for the journey when they were finally apprehended in Tipton two days later.

The presence of Germans in the Shrewsbury camp caused antagonism right from the start. Inevitably prisoners wanted to make the best of their situation and in December 1914 the prisoners decided that they would hold a concert with the intention of using it as a means of raising some spare cash for necessities – by this time there were between 500 and 600 prisoners in the camp. Officials in the War Office came to hear of the plans and vetoed the concert which led to a spate of correspondence in the *Chronicle*. The commandant of the camp began it by writing a letter to the mayor regretting the decision because, as he said:

'I am sorry to learn that the permission which I have given to the prisoners of war in this camp to give a small concert within the precincts of their enclosure has given offence to some residents in Shrewsbury. The facts are that these soldiers are destitute of everything but the uniform they were wearing and which they had been wearing since August. It was my duty to see that such articles of clothing as were necessary for their health and cleanliness were supplied, but they were without money to buy tobacco or comforts or to supplement their daily ration. The idea of a concert had, therefore, a two-fold object – one to collect a little money for their benefit, the second to provide them with occupation in preparing for it. I am sorry anyone should think there is harm in this.'

In the following week's paper there was an article concerning the banned concert by a reporter who had been to the camp to interview the commandant. He reported that the commandant had received many letters from members of the public and

'for the most part [these] were from broad-minded people who seemed to wonder that anybody should grumble about the staff doing their best for the people in their charge according to the rules of the Hague Convention. Practically all the letters were from English people, some of whom have sons fighting at the front against the Germans. On the other hand a few letters, for the most part anonymous, abusing the Germans, have been received.'

Included with some of the letters were donations of money for the prisoners so that at the end the commandant said he didn't think the prisoners would be the losers.

But that wasn't the end of it. Some German ladies who lived in Shrewsbury decided to take matters into their own hands and personally delivered to the prisoners a Christmas tree 'illuminated and decorated in typical German style' along with a number of gifts. That might have gone unnoticed except that one of the ladies made herself unpopular with the guards when, having given her (more generous) gifts to the prisoners she then rather facetiously handed to the guards a 'penny packet of Woodbines'.

Meantime, the vicar of St Mary's church had expressed his sympathy to the prisoners which resulted in a letter to the *Chronicle* that can only be described as vitriolic. The correspondent, who signed himself as 'Disgusted' wrote:

'I suppose the Vicar has read the reports of the horrible and ghastly atrocities committed by the Germans in the early part of the war. May I suggest to him that at the moment there may be, and very probably are, many of the men who committed, participated, or connived at these awful deeds in the camp? Is it, therefore, to these men, that the Vicar asks us to extend our sympathy? It appears to many others and myself, that through the unaccountably ridiculous behaviour of a few people who demurred at the concert being abandoned, and then "poured gifts" upon the prisoners, that a stigma was placed upon Shrewsbury. Therefore, if the Vicar and these few misguided people cannot keep their view and their sympathy to themselves let them pack up and clear out, or join the German army and the people of Shrewsbury will be relieved of the taint of Pro-Germanism.'

But it wasn't just the Germans who became prisoners of war. Many Shrewsbury men found themselves in similar camps in Germany and, before long, people who had been notified that their menfolk were imprisoned began to send parcels to them. Such parcels were delivered largely through the Red Cross and contained all manner of items. It is interesting to note, though, that in July 1915 a notice was placed in all the newspapers advising the public not to send tin parcels to prisoners of war in Germany. By this time metals were becoming scarce; they were needed for munitions and other military purposes and the authorities were well aware that this was not a problem that was confined to the allies. In Germany there was just the same desperate need for metals so that tin boxes being used to carry gifts for prisoners often never got to their destination. The notice therefore advised anyone sending a parcel to Germany that all such parcels should be packed in strong wooden or double cardboard boxes.

Letters started to arrive from prisoners asking for particular items and so it was not long before different regiments (or at least the wives of regimental commanders) began to set up charities to organize the collection and distribution of the items and advertisements and letters began to appear in the papers asking for help. They were asking for everything – from second-hand boots to belts, shaving items and soap, food and tobacco.

One lady wrote to the *Chronicle* detailing just what kind of clothing was needed:

'In view of the approaching cold weather may I venture to suggest what a blessing it would be to the British prisoners of war in Germany to receive some warm woollen under-clothing? I understand new undergarments are often appropriated by the Germans, but part worn things never are. If any such are sent to me, clean and mended, I will most gladly undertake to send them to some of the Detention camps, for the leading NCOs to distribute. Flannel shirts, woollen pants and vests and socks are specially useful; also I believe old tennis or canvas shoes of any kind are most acceptable, as the men often get sprained ankles from wearing the clogs supplied to them by the Germans. No cotton articles should be sent, and only black suits and overcoats.'

The Committee of the KSLI Prisoners of War Fund, for example, asked people (or towns or villages) to adopt prisoners. The figures make interesting reading (especially these days). The Fund provided every Shropshire prisoner in Germany with three food parcels per fortnight, each of which cost 7s 6d. The parcels contained 2lbs of meat, one tin of fish, oatmeal, bread, jam or syrup, margarine or dripping, chocolate, soups, tea, sugar, milk and soap. And, of course, smokes. Clothing was also sent so that each year a prisoner would get two pairs of boots, two pairs of shoes, six pairs of socks, four pairs of drawers, four vests, four shirts, two pairs of trousers, two jackets, two cardigans, two pairs of gloves, four towels, six handkerchiefs, two caps, two kitbags, wool and darning needles, one great coat and one pair of braces.

As the war progressed the supply of food became increasing problematic and with less and less men in the workforce at home it was inevitable that at some point the use of prisoners of war to help in the fields would be considered. The War Office found that most farmers were only too pleased to make use of such a labour force so that in March 1917 notices were placed in many newspapers serving rural districts that:

'Any person wishing to be supplied with prisoner of war labour should send an early application to The Commandant, Prisoner of War Camp, Shrewsbury. Preference will be given to Employers requiring Labour for urgent national purposes, notably agriculture, including vegetable gardening ... Employers will be required to pay for this labour at the current local rate of wages, and to give a guarantee that Compensation for injury or death up to the maximum payable under the Workmen's Compensation Act will be paid by the employer. This labour can only be supplied in the vicinity of Shrewsbury, at such a distance as will permit the prisoners of war returning daily to the Internment Camp. Such labour will be liable to withdrawal at one week's notice.'

Not all work was of an agricultural nature. One prisoner died in the military hospital at Berrington having been injured when working in a local quarry.

There's always someone, of course, who will cheat the system so that it's amusing to note a complaint in the *Chronicle* when someone (nameless) asks 'Is it true that a poor allotment holder in Shrewsbury, who gets his potatoes at a reduced rate, can afford to engage four Germans and their guards daily to cultivate his plot?'

By 1918, however, there was less and less food to go round. The situation was bad enough in Britain but at least some convoys were getting through to supply the country with food. In Germany, where the blockade of the country's ports was much more effective, the situation was far far worse and ordinary people were, quite literally, starving. So, too, were the prisoners of war. One such prisoner, Corporal F.T. Worrall of the Coldstream Guards, sent home to Shrewsbury a letter in which he described the daily ration for the prisoners 'in those barbed wire hells' who did not get food parcels. It was written in 1916 and makes bleak reading:

'Breakfast [consisted of] acorn coffee, no milk and no sugar, tastes like warm ink, slice of evil looking sour black bread, about five by four inches and ½ inch thick. Dinner... greasy looking hot water, supposed to be soup with perhaps a potato or two in it. Tea... acorn coffee and another slice of bread, same dimensions as breakfast. Sometimes a little barley boiled in water is given or else meal, such as is given to dogs, with small apples, good and bad, boiled and mixed up. Would any person living in Salop care to exist on meals of this kind? If parcels are not sent then this is the routine which each prisoner will have to face every day.'

Corporal Worrall went on to say 'In the earlier days of the war, before parcels commenced to reach us, most of us were forced by hunger to search in dustbins and swill tubs for anything we could find to eat, and we tried to sleep to forget our hungry stomachs. We exchanged our khaki with French prisoners, who were getting parcels, for anything we could get to eat.'

(Incidentally, in December 1918 there is an advertisement in the *Chronicle* for a lost item to be returned which reads: 'Lost on 2nd December last, a Soldier's Discharge Silver Badge. Finder rewarded on returning same to FT Worrall, Borough Police Station, Shrewsbury.' I wonder if he ever got it back.)

Chapter Seventeen

Peace at Last

BY THE MIDDLE of 1918 there began to be a strong feeling amongst people generally that the war would soon come to an end. Both sides were worn out and everyone knew it; it just couldn't go on much longer. But despite this anticipation of the end, no-one could be sure when it would happen. The 'over by Christmas' anticipation that so many had felt when the war began was now something that no-one dared to hope for.

Hopes, however, began to rise, and in many ways this affected life styles generally despite such things as food and other rationing which got steadily worse. People began to look to a time when the country was no longer at war. It was evident by then that, once the war was over, Home Rule for Ireland would once again be on the agenda and in Shropshire there was talk of a similar deal for Wales. In April 1918 a conference was held in Shrewsbury on this very subject where, believe it or not, it was even mooted by some that Shrewsbury would be an ideal capital once Wales became independent.

Not everyone anticipated a return to the good life. Some could see the thorns amongst the future's roses leading to a comment in the *Chronicle* which warned that 'during the war, as during previous wars, employment is abundant, and money is plentiful. The nation is living on its capital. It is borrowing at a high rate, and living on borrowed money. Inevitably there must be a bad time coming. Great wars are always followed by industrial depression, by lack of employment, want, and distress; and this is the greatest of all wars.'

As the end of the war approached there were also discussions as to how to treat with Germany once peace was declared. Feelings ran high. At a meeting (of the UK Commercial Travellers Association) in Shrewsbury in September 1918 a resolution was passed in which it was agreed that 'we exclude for twenty-five years from the date of

The Square.

declaration of peace any German from membership, and we will boycott by all means in our power all production of German origin'.

But still no-one knew when the war would end. In fact, just as in the weeks before the declaration of war, events moved with a suddenness that surprised everyone. Russia, of course, had long since made terms with Germany but in the east fighting had continued elsewhere so that when the Turks surrendered in the Holy Land this was marked by a thanksgiving service in St Mary's Church at the beginning of October. By now notes were being exchanged between the western governments and Germany with the latter seeking terms that were as favourable as possible whilst the west wanted an agreement that would ensure Germany's full surrender.

And then on 4 November Austria-Hungary agreed to an armistice, leaving Germany on its own. This was followed four days later when Kaiser Wilhelm was forced to abdicate and a German republic was proclaimed. So it was with this new republic that the armistice of 11 November was agreed. Initially the armistice was only for a period of thirty-six days but when the news came out everyone ignored that minor detail. And, anyhow, the terms were such that Germany would have found it virtually impossible to start fighting again once the thirty-six days were passed.

In Shrewsbury, even before the news was actually confirmed, people were aware that it was about to happen. The agreement was finalized some six hours beforehand, so that by 8.00 am that morning people in Shrewsbury were already gathering in the Square awaiting the official confirmation. Shortly after noon the Mayor, Samuel Meakin Morris, made an official announcement from the steps of the Guildhall and this was followed by boys from Shrewsbury School playing bugles and drums. The whole town erupted with the excitement of the news, with soldiers from surrounding camps coming into Shrewsbury to join in the celebrations and a band coming in from the airfield at Shawbury to play through the streets.

But despite the general jubilation, not everyone was rejoicing. Up and down the country there were families who had only just received news of the deaths of loved ones and in the days that followed many more were to suffer in the same way. One family in Shrewsbury who got the news that very day was, of course, the family of the poet, Wilfred Owen.

It was not just war casualties that was causing grief either. The Spanish flu epidemic had already taken hold. This was an international disaster. The fighting during the First World War had changed the picture of warfare for ever. Such were the machines of war that, for the first time in history, deaths in battle exceeded deaths from battlefield diseases and poor hygiene. But, although numbers will never be accurately counted, the death toll from the flu epidemic undoubtedly killed far more people than all the Great War battles added together.

In Shrewsbury the epidemic had struck in the middle of October. At first no-one realised just how bad it was so that although several primary schools were closed and the authorities in local military camps put the cinemas and public houses 'out of bounds' for their men, there was still a complaint by men who worked at the Army Pay Corps offices in town, for example, that whilst they couldn't go to the theatre the lady clerks who worked alongside them could do so.

By the beginning of November the death toll in Shrewsbury was rising. Many more schools closed their doors (which, of course, meant that when the armistice was declared those children who were well enough to enjoy the festivities could do so without complaint from adults!) as did the theatre and other places of entertainment. At Shrewsbury School over 200 boys went down with influenza. Inevitably this all meant that the medical profession was hard-pressed to keep up with the work. One effect of this was that those doctors who worked for the Army Recruiting Service cancelled all medical examinations of men who had just been called up – it's interesting to note that even in the week before the war ended, nothing had yet been done to stop the recruiting process.

Previous influenza epidemics had tended to cause most deaths amongst the elderly. Although it certainly killed many elderly people, this epidemic, however, seemed mostly to effect young people and those who would normally have been considered to be in good health. And it killed quickly – one young Shrewsbury woman, aged only twenty-seven, died within a day or so of contracting the illness.

Fortunately, the weather turned colder in the middle of November and the virulence of the epidemic declined – in Shrewsbury at least.

The Spanish Flu epidemic wasn't, however, the only medical problem that affected people in the months that followed the armistice. With so many men returning from the battlefields the population had to be warned of another serious problem – the presence of venereal diseases amongst the men. There were regular warnings concerning the risks from such diseases and people were told not only about the clinics that were being set up in towns around the country, but also advised that this was not necessarily the result of immorality.

'Though it is "after the war"' as one article in the paper put it, 'there is a danger threatening old England and her men and women and boys and girls, and her unborn children, with as deadly a peril to life and happiness as ever came from German shell or bomb.

'Every year, in normal times, there are about 300,000 fresh cases of Venereal Diseases (Syphilis and Gonorrhoea). After a war, history has always shown that the numbers go up by leaps and bounds and the disease is often spread to country districts where it has hitherto been almost unknown.

'One quarter of all the blindness in the country is due to Venereal Disease, and sometimes insanity and paralysis are due to the same cause, as well as the loss of thousands of infant lives through miscarriages and stillbirths. It is known, too, that much of the infection is of an innocent nature and is not the result of immorality.

'Much has already been done towards breaking down the conspiracy of silence

Shrewsbury School.

which has helped so largely towards the ravages of this "hidden plague". False modesty, which has withheld from children a healthy knowledge of the facts of life, taught as only parents can really teach them, with love and reverence, has sent our boys and girls out into the world defenceless against temptation and the suggestive glamour of the unknown. Knowledge is power and the old assumption that ignorance must be innocence is responsible for countless cases of Venereal Disease'.

It wasn't just men and prisoners (over 50,000 prisoners of war had already reached England by the beginning of December) who came home. Horses did, too. And many were sold in the market in Shrewsbury. The first such sale took place in the week before Christmas with 150 'surplus animals' including 'eight heavy draught, 107 light draught, and 33 riding horses'. The following week a further 600 horses were put up for sale. Bear in mind, as you read these numbers, that this is just two sales in one country town – it makes one gasp to consider that some 65,000 horses were being sold altogether throughout the country at this time, not to mention those of poorer quality that were put down in France.

After the Second World War rationing of foodstuffs continued for almost another ten years so that it comes as a surprise to see that within two weeks of the armistice an announcement was made ending the rationing of tea. Then the beginning of January saw the announcement that, as from February, there would be an increase in the ration for sugar from 1/2lb to 3/4lb and there were also plans to de-ration jam and margarine soon.

So life, in some respects was quickly returning to normal and to emphasize this fact, no sooner had the armistice been declared than another announcement was made – this time that an election would be held almost immediately. The election was to be held on 14 December and, immediately, candidates started to canvas the people with their addresses being printed in the paper. Those anti-German sentiments once again came to the fore, with many people insisting on knowing before they voted just what their candidates views were on what was to be done not just about the peace plans with Germany but also regarding any German people who already lived in Britain or wanted to come here.

This was also the first election in which women could vote although it applied only to those who were aged over thirty; it took another ten years before the age was dropped for all men and women aged twenty-one. The bill that enfranchised women had been passed earlier that same year and it was generally agreed that the women had earned their right to have a say in how the country was run. Not that they, or the men, made a particularly good choice on this occasion – Lloyd George, won the election with promises that Britain would be a 'land fit for heroes' but, once in power, he promptly reneged on many of his election promises and, as that writer to the *Chronicle* some months before had warned, a 'bad time followed by industrial depression, lack of employment and distress' was certainly coming.

Chapter Eighteen

Shrewsbury's War Memorials

LONG BEFORE THE war ended memorial services were being held and physical memorials were being produced. The first services tended to be held each year on the anniversary of the outbreak of the war and many were almost martial in aspect with the *Chronicle* in 1916, for example, stating that demonstrations would be held throughout the Empire on 4 August 'to emphasize the resolve of the people to prosecute hostilities until victory has been obtained'. But this attitude was not always dominant and from very early on in the war such services became more services of remembrance for those who had died. Inevitably collections would be made during these services in support of such things as the Red Cross or St Dunstan's Hospital for the Blind.

It wasn't long, also, before physical memorials were being produced – particularly in those parts of the country that had suffered through the loss of so many local men. One such area was the Castlefields district in Shrewsbury. It was there that the first shrine in the town was erected in November 1916 and it listed the seventy men from just three streets (New Park Street, Lindley Street and Victoria Terrace) who had joined up. Three of them had been killed. Soon afterwards another shrine was raised in the same district, this time recalling men from nearby John Street and, within a year, a third was dedicated remembering the men of Queen Street. Once the war was over the shrines were moved into All Saints Church where they were later replaced by a larger alabaster memorial which lists the seventy-nine men of the parish who were killed.

Nearby is St Michael's Church, now used as a Masonic Hall, and outside the building stands its memorial with seventy-two names. On this memorial there are four surnames the same – Clift, three of whom were brothers. So many from one family was by no means unusual. One family, for example, in Church Stretton had already, by the end of 1914, seventeen sons who had joined up, fourteen of whom, even then, were at the front. This was an age before contraception was the norm yet with improved

War memorial by the Masonic Hall.

War memorial on Platform Three, Shrewsbury Station.

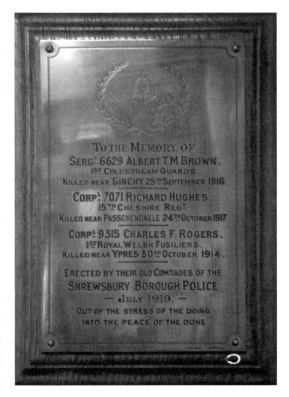

health and hygiene leading to the survival of many more of the babies that were born – large families were the norm.

The full casualty figures for the First World War will probably never be known. British Empire losses alone amounted to over three million. Just over twelve per cent of the total number of British soldiers who served in France and Belgium died, with an additional thirty-eight per cent wounded. That means that half of all the soldiers who went to the western front could expect to become casualties of one sort or another. It's no wonder that there's hardly a church in the country that doesn't have a memorial listing names of those who were lost. Indeed, in the entire country there were only thirty-two villages in which all the men who joined up returned. They came

War memorial in Monkmoor Road Police Station.

to be known as *Thankful Villages*, the only one in Shropshire being the village of Harley.

It is not just in churches that one finds these memorials. In Shrewsbury there are three memorials at Shrewsbury Station dedicated to those men who had worked for the London and North Western and the Great Western Joint Railways before they joined up. The only one of the three memorials in a public place sits, not in an obvious place like the entrance hall to the station, but on Platform Three and gives forty-two names. Altogether more than 25,000 Great Western railwaymen joined up and some ten per cent of them gave their lives.

Similarly there is a memorial in the town's police headquarters on Monkmoor Road to those three policemen from the town who were killed. Men of the highest rank were amongst those who died – the Chief Constable of the Shropshire was amongst them. Gerard Lysley Derriman had been educated at Eton after which he joined the Grenadier Guards and subsequently served in the Boer War. Leaving the army he was appointed as Chief Constable of Shropshire in 1908 but then, once the war broke out, he resigned and rejoined his old regiment which perhaps explains why he is not named on the memorial. Captain Derriman died as a result of wounds received in France in August 1915.

Memorials of this type tend to be a reasonably complete list of names of those who lost their lives since it was relatively easy when preparing the memorial to check through company registers. On the other hand, memorials in churches and other more public places do not necessarily list all those in the parish or the general locality. This was because it was usually up to the family members of anyone who died to apply for their son's, husband's, brother's name to be included and it is worth bearing this fact in mind when searching for names on such memorials.

Perhaps this also explains why, on a memorial in St George's Church in Frankwell, the name of Private Denis Blakemore is included. His is perhaps one of the saddest memorials because he was shot at dawn in July 1917, having been found guilty of desertion. Three hundred and forty-six soldiers were shot by firing squad in the Great War, and nearly all of them, like Private Blakemore, were suffering from shellshock. However, in a surprisingly sympathetic move on the part of the military authorities at the time, in most cases their families were informed that their loved ones had been 'killed in action'. This being the case they would naturally have wanted their names

**Shot at Dawn, The National Memorial
Arboretum, Alrewas. Staffs.**
(Amanda Robertson)

Memorial in St George's Church, Frankwell that names Private Blakemore.

TO THE GLORY OF GOD, AND IN GRATEFUL
MEMORY OF THOSE BRAVE MEN WHO LEFT THIS
PARISH, AND GAVE THEIR LIVES FOR THEIR
COUNTRY IN THE GREAT WAR.

"BE THOU FAITHFUL UNTO DEATH, AND I WILL
GIVE THEE A CROWN OF LIFE."

Capt G.E. JOHNSON	Driv. H.BRADDICK	Pte E.KILLAN
R.E.RUMSEY	A.C.JONES	H.G.LAMBERT
Lieut G.H.MORLEY	S.spr. J.B.MILLER	W.LAW
2ND A.PRICE	D.R.MORGAN	C.E.LINES
G.C.WRIGHT	Pion. R.A.DAWES	E.N.MANSELL
Sgt.Maj. R.W.BURBRIDGE	Priv. A.ACHWOOD	C.H.MEREDITH
S.R.BILL	W.E.BATES	W.MERRIFIELD
Sergt C.A.COX	S.BECKWORTH	A.B.MILNER
J.B.LLOYD	D.J.BLAKEMORE	W.H.MILNER
E.A.POWELL	W.BRAY	H.MORGAN
W.PALMER	H.J.BROOKES	R.E.MOORE
Ft.Sgt. W.B.ROBERTS	C.E.BURGWIN	J.W.MORLEY
L.Sgt. W.H.J.FERRETT	A.CARTWRIGHT	G.PEEL
A.LLOYD	C.DAVIES	W.PEEL
Corp. W.G.MANSELL	F.DAVIES	P.H.PRICE
F.BROWN	R.W.DAWES	T.H.ROBERTS
J.W.PRICE	R.C.DUDLEY	L.ROBERTS
I.A.SMITH	R.J.EASTHOPE	T.SIMMONDS
L.Cpl. H.EBREY	T.H.EVANS	W.H.SPENCER
G.F.EVANS	P.EVANS	A.G.SALMON
T.L.PEEL	A.GRADY	P.E SMITH
W.A.MEREDITH	R.GROOM	F.J.SUTTON
T.W.PURSLOW	C.HANNANT	P.WALLEY
C.E.SPENCER	W.HILTON	T.P.WARHAM
J.W.WALKER	J.H.JONES	J.A.WENLOCK
Yeo or Sig. S. J.F.FERRETT	R.A.JONES	G.H.WENLOCK
Gun. R.BROWN	A.JONES	W.R.WELSBY
D.CROSS	L.JONES	T.WYATT
G.A.RICHARDS	S.N.JUCKES	2Cpl F.MEREDITH

The unveiling of the Shrewsbury School war memorial in July 1923. Notice the seats to the right which were reserved for relatives of those who had died. *(Shrewsbury School)*

included in local memorials. These men were battlefield victims, too.

Some of the most poignant memorials are those in schools; this is perhaps because these memorials, particularly, remind us that it was a generation that was lost. School memorials tend to be complete insofar as they list all the boys from that school who lost their lives. The best known school memorial in Shrewsbury is the one in the grounds of Shrewsbury School. But the School did not wait until the end of the war before remembering its losses. In March 1918 a special memorial service was held in the chapel to remember the first hundred Old Salopians who had given their lives and soon afterwards plans were in progress to raise funds for a permanent memorial. By August of that year some £8,000 had already been subscribed. In all some £16,000 was raised, far more than was needed for the statue. Consequently the additional money was used for other memorials with much of it being reserved to pay for the education of the sons of those old boys who had been killed.

Boys such as those from Shrewsbury School joined up in their thousands when war was first declared, most of them immediately being entrusted with officer status and therefore inevitably amongst the first to be killed once they went into battle. The roll call

Sir Philip Sidney.

for Shrewsbury School mirrors that of such schools up and down the country – some 1,850 former pupils (and masters) served in the First World War with 321 being killed.

One boy who was at Shrewsbury School when the war broke out was the future novelist Nevil Shute. Leaving school in 1916 he then served as a soldier in the Suffolk Regiment. In his biography he recalled the mood in the school during those early years of the war when:

> 'the list of casualties grew every day. Older boys that we knew intimately left, appeared once or twice resplendent in new uniforms, and [then] were dead. We remembered them as we had known them less than a year before, as we knelt praying for their souls in the chapel, knowing as we did so that in a year or so the little boys… would be kneeling for us'.

Incidentally, the statue standing on the plinth shows Sir Philip Sidney who attended the school in the mid-1500s. Although he is shown wearing a breastplate he is without his cuisses (thigh armour). This is because before the Battle of Zutphen in 1586 he loaned this armour to a friend and so had no protection when he was later hit in his thigh by a musket ball. The wound festered and he died a month later. Tradition has it that, as he was returning, wounded, to the camp he was offered a drink of water but noticed another wounded soldier looking longingly towards the cup. 'Give the drink to that soldier,' Sidney said, indicating the man, 'His need is greater than mine.' It is this scene that is shown in one of the plaques on the memorial.

The Philip Sidney memorial is not the only memorial at Shrewsbury School. Another is the Boat House. It was built in memory of John Edwin Pugh who, as a pupil, had rowed for the school. During the war he served in the newly-formed RAF. The boathouse was built with money donated by his father, the owner of a motorcycle manufacturing

Plaque on the Sidney memorial showing the scene where Sidney gives his water to another wounded soldier.

Shrewsbury School boat house.

The temporary memorial outside the library. *(David Benson)*

company. John Pugh was one of the many who went straight from school to war; he was still only aged nineteen when he died on 12 November 1918, the day after the armistice was declared, from wounds that he had received just beforehand.

In 1919, as the anniversary of the armistice approached, a suggestion was made that a three minute silence should be held at 11.00 am on 11 November to honour those who had been killed. The idea rapidly took hold so that the entire country came to a halt that day.

Already in Shrewsbury a memorial, not just for the county's dead but for all who had served in some way, had been erected in front of the Library. It was dedicated on 5 August 1919 and all the town had closed down. Despite the seriousness of the occasion the event was almost a gala day with people coming into the town from all over the county. This was only a temporary structure in the form of a cross about ten feet in height with a base which was soon surrounded by wreathes and other flowers.

It wasn't until 29 July 1922 that the permanent memorial for those in Shropshire who died in the Great War was unveiled. This memorial stands in the Quarry Gardens and depicts a statue of St Michael, the patron saint of warriors, a lance in his left hand whilst

The dedication ceremony at the war memorial in the Quarry, remembering all those from Shropshire who died in the First World War. *(David Benson)*

holding his right hand out as though giving a blessing. Like the statue of Philip Sidney at Shrewsbury School the money to erect this memorial was raised by public subscription and, again as with the Sidney statue, people were generous to a fault so that there was enough spare cash left over with which to build an extension to the Royal Salop Infirmary. This was opened in 1927 providing, in the new wing, twenty-two beds for children and eight maternity beds.

Sadly, virtually all those memorials that were produced to remember those who gave their lives in the Great War had additional names added less than thirty years later. Little can Marshal Foch of France have known just how percipient his words were when, in June 1919, he said:

'This is not peace. It is an armistice for twenty years.'

Acknowledgements for Illustrations

All illustrations used in this book come from the author's own collection, unless credited in the caption. The author wishes to thank the generosity of those who have given permission for their pictures to be used.

Index